Take Action

Anthony Joseph

PASSIONPRENEUR®
PUBLISHING

Take Action

Anthony Joseph

PASSIONPRENEUR®
P U B L I S H I N G

Publishing information
Publishing and design facilitated by
Passionpreneur Publishing,
A division of Passionpreneur Organization Pty Ltd,
ABN: 48640637529

Melbourne, VIC | Australia
www.PassionpreneurPublishing.com

Table of Contents

I dedicate this book to my late father, Dr. Joseph Antoine Abou Jaoude, who taught almost four thousand students over fifteen years at the University of Notre Dame and other universities. He was one of my first inspirations in life. I hope he is looking down on me from the heavens, proud of the man I have become.

Acknowledgments

I would like to acknowledge Moustafa Hamwi and his entire team who helped me to write this book, including Clare McIvor, Cat Martindale-Vale, and Shobha Nihalani.

To my grandfather, Judge and author Kamil Saleme, for being a huge inspiration in my life and a great example to follow.

To my grandmother, Josephine Saleme, for always being there and making things easier and great.

For my mother, Claudine Saleme, who accepted me for who I am, always stood by me in the good and the bad, always took care of me, and loved me unconditionally.

To my Uncle, Piere Saleme, and his, Mrs. Beguita, for having me in Dubai and supporting me in the early years of my endeavors.

To my brother, Roy Abou Jaoude, for his endless support.

To my wife and my rock, Joy Abou Jaoude, for being my backbone and my backstage support and for always making me a better person.

To my brother-in-law, Roy El Baba, and my sister-in-law, Rita Abou Jaoude, for their true love and constant support.

To my brother and business partner, Loai Al Fakir, for inspiring me, supporting me from the start, and believing in me when I didn't.

To my brother, Sinan Sami, for loving me and being unconditionally there on the good and bad days.

To all my friends, supporters, and followers, for always making me feel special and giving me the feeling that I am changing the world, bit by bit. You are the reason I do what I do, and I will keep doing it as long as I breathe.

CHAPTER 1
TAKE ACTION

It was the year 2020, and the world had been waiting for it. It seemed like a beautiful number, implying a fresh start full of hope and blessings—a new beginning.

None of us ever imagined that what would follow was even possible. How could such a profound and widespread disaster even exist? It hadn't happened in living memory and hadn't happened in over one hundred years.

A pandemic.

What in the hell is that?

The repercussions hit in a tsunami of restrictions. Quarantines, lockdowns, and vaccines—all of these were new words for me, and I am sure that was the case for many of you as well. Fear was thick in the air. Everyone was panicking.

Is this it? Is this the end of the world?

Ever since I was a child, I heard that the end was near and that we should pray for forgiveness every day so our souls could go to the heavens. All those stories started in 1999 when people said our computers and calendars would crash and that we wouldn't be able to adapt to the new era. No one had the technology to foretell what would happen as the clock ticked over at the stroke of midnight that New Year's Eve. We waited for calamity, but nothing out of the ordinary happened. Everything was normal. Life continued and even became better.

The same panic returned in 2012 when the talk of the end of the world arose again. There were movies made about it. Again, life continued, economies were doing great, many countries flourished, and most importantly, technologies served humans and enhanced their lives. What a beautiful world to be in!

By 2020, most humans on the planet were connected through the internet, web applications, or telecommunications platforms. Who would have ever thought that a day would come when any human could connect with another by a simple text message or what we call a direct message—or DM—in our modern language?

The nature of human beings is to be innovative. We, as human beings, always look to better ourselves in search of a better life.

However, what was certain was that no one had ever imagined a pandemic, much less prepared for it. Life as we knew it didn't exist anymore. The most annoying part was that there were no indications of where life was taking us.

I still remember that day in my office when I received the call that said we would have a lockdown very soon. I didn't expect that to ever actually happen.

Suddenly, on March 17, 2020, it was announced that Dubai was going to have a lockdown until further notice. The pandemic became a reality. I will never forget my wife's face when I reached home. She was anxious and worried. I immediately comforted her with a hug and said, "Don't worry. I'm sure it's temporary, and everything will go back to normal very soon."

To be honest, that was the first time I felt a sense of uncertainty about what tomorrow had in store for me. I didn't know what I was going to do other than research what this pandemic was all about, how long it would last, what caused it to happen, and how to survive it.

The last time there was a global pandemic was the Spanish flu in 1918, which lasted four years. This time, it was different. Global transportation enabled the virus to spread faster, and soon no country had been left untouched. The lockdowns seemed to stretch on indefinitely.

What was COVID-19? Was it lethal? I wanted to know more about this invisible enemy. I started reading article after article, but no article was like the other. Some said it was airborne, some said it spread through touch, some said it could survive on any surface for twenty-four hours, some even said it only targeted the elderly, while some said everyone was in danger. The central message was to stay home and not meet anyone.

I told my wife that I had been researching for over two hours, and it was clear that no one knew anything. I couldn't find even two articles that shared the same information. I reassured her that everyone was speculating and that, no matter what happened, we didn't need to worry. We could afford to be indoors, even if we didn't work for a few years. What was really important was to stay at home, stay safe, and not visit anyone or let anyone come over.

The government had announced that we needed to submit a permit request to leave the house. We had to state our reason for leaving the house, such as for medical purposes or grocery shopping. The request would be reviewed, and we would receive an approval or rejection within minutes. Luckily, we had a huge Spinneys store just across the road from our house, so we could buy whatever we wanted within walking distance. I felt so much better shopping for groceries. Spending those twenty minutes outside my home felt good, but then I would return to my kitchen to the updates and news. I would scroll through Facebook and Instagram, then kill the night with a Netflix series.

A few days later, I started feeling that my energy levels were going down. The news was terrible. Hundreds of thousands of new COVID-19 cases were mentioned every day. There was news of people dying, people losing jobs, and businesses shutting down. No matter what I was watching or reading, the news was depressing.

What really affected me were the changes happening to my routine and my body, which also affected my mood. I am not the kind of man to sit around. Both mentally and physically, I am a man of action.

Before the COVID-19 lockdown, I trained every morning before work, then spent twelve hours being very active and returned home.

During lockdown, all of that was gone. The lack of exercise began to affect me mentally and physically. I even stopped eating clean and filled my day with junk food and unhealthy snacks. My mind was filled with negative news and mindless TV.

After two weeks, I had enough. I decided to stop listening to the news and tried to keep my mind clear. I wanted to be away from the negativity and put all my energy into useful action. That's when I decided to take action.

The Take Action mentality is a way to break out of a negative loop. If you feel you are falling into the trap of negativity, it's time to get a grip on reality and discipline yourself. You are responsible for yourself. No one will do it for you. You have to develop that willpower to take charge of your life.

I recall the old days when I arrived in Dubai with nothing—no money or resources. I felt like I was this tiny object in this huge world. I was in survival mode, and the willpower to make something out of myself was great. Bit by bit, I built myself up into who I am today.

I took charge of my life.

The way to achieve this was to have the right attitude and the hunger to prove something, to break through the ceiling I created for myself.

I heard this quote: "You are your own worst enemy and your own best friend." I realized you have to think about whom you feed: the enemy or the friend.

Looking back to the beginning of my real estate journey, Dubai wasn't on the plan.

When I first came to Dubai in October 2014, it was to visit my uncle. To be honest, that was when I fell in love with the city. We were driving down the main highway, Sheikh Zayed Road, and I saw all these high-rise buildings. I was like, "Wow, that's gorgeous." That's when I had this hunch—this inner voice—that told me to stay no matter what.

My uncle said to me, "You know what? You're really good at sales. Why don't you apply for a real estate job?"

And that's what I did. I sent my CV to fifteen companies. Within two days, they started calling me. I went for interviews. "When can you start?" was the fantastic response.

Again, my instincts guided me. Many of these big companies were big and flashy, but some were fishy. I chose a smaller company with only thirty staff; the office was about one thousand square feet. I started working there. It was hard work. I had little or no training, and

I had to figure out how to get clients. I listened to the other brokers, but it was getting harder and harder with all the competition.

It wasn't actually in my plan to be there. You can say it was fate or the universe guiding me toward my destiny. I stayed there and learned a lot about myself and the world.

Since then, I have never looked back. I struggled, but I took charge of my life and made it work.

I was aware that, in every single moment, I had a choice: to take action or stay passive. I realized this choice decides our destiny.

One must not be afraid of hard work. Trust yourself and go forward to take action. Prove to yourself that you can become successful in your goal.

My first book—Take Charge—detailed my journey to become the ideal real estate broker. This was someone who could stand out in the crowd and wanted to develop themselves into someone who took the work seriously and acted ethically.

Take Action is for everyone. No matter what you are selling, you need to transform into someone with the values and character of an entrepreneur. Values drive your goal. They enable you to face challenges and focus on your inner guide.

My point is that anyone who wants to be an entrepreneur or start their own company or service will recognize the value of Take Action.

So let me share with you my secrets to taking action.

CHAPTER 2
THE PIVOTING ACTION

"You are not a tree.
If you don't like where you are: move."

– Jim Rohn

The first thing anyone must have in life is passion—
passion for their product. In that context, my
passion was the real estate of Dubai. I was in awe of this
megacity. It was the best place on the planet to invest
and the most underrated.

The deeper I got into my business, the more I started
understanding the value of this city. The fact was that
Dubai's properties were extremely affordable, with no

tax, and anyone could get a mortgage. So I looked at this massive opportunity to share this with the world.

In April 2020, while we were still in the pandemic, there were many people who felt they were victims. They had millions of excuses to do nothing. However, playing the blame game is not a way of living. That is not how I think or function. Yes, it was a fact: we were in bad times. I thought to myself, "It is what it is." We needed to learn to adapt. New times meant new perspectives. I chose to look for the silver lining in every dark cloud.

When the COVID-19 pandemic started, it was the end of my last roadshow in the UK. There was a group of us. We returned to Dubai on March 11, 2020. On March 17, we got the notice that everything was shut down, and we were told to sit at home.

In a matter of two days, I started losing my mind. I simply cannot sit still mentally or physically. It is not in my nature. That's when I started writing my first book, Take Charge.

During that time of lockdown, after I came to terms with the situation, I began to think of other ways that

I could do business. I was keeping myself updated with the news of the world, not of COVID-19.

If you notice certain people's behavior, you will see that in a crisis, most people tend to be dramatic and say that life is over, but other types of people have the opposite reaction. They find the opportunity and make the best of any situation.

I chose to be the latter.

I didn't dwell on what was going wrong. I began to focus on the future and how to make it right.

That's when I started to take action.

That made me super busy. How?

I found an opportunity in the most unusual way.

The developers in Dubai needed buyers and were willing to accept different payment methods. I found a way to get that to work. We started calling developers we knew had connections in Lebanon, which was experiencing economic turmoil.

The Lebanese banks had imposed controls that made it difficult for millions of customers to withdraw their money from their accounts. If any local wanted to withdraw money from their account, they were only allowed a limited amount. The value of the Lebanese pound plunged, and many Lebanese people sought export-focused companies to get something from the "trapped" money.[1]

I convinced the developers to sell and accept the payment through a manager's check from a Lebanese bank. We registered the properties in Dubai. It was an ideal situation for the developers and enabled protection for the buyers. It was amazing. Despite the lockdown, we were on the phone all day, making money. I didn't even need to step out of my house. Sitting around at home, even in my underwear, I was making these calls!

Leads were raining in. That filled my day with an easy fifteen hours of talking and explaining to people how it works, and it worked like magic. Many Lebanese people were keen to get back their money through property investments. This was an opportunity for them to

---

[1] https://www.reuters.com/world/middle-east/financial-surrealism-lebanese-opt-beer-over-banks-2021-06-17/

invest in a city that offered great value. After a couple of weeks, the projects were all sold out. Everyone was locked at home, so I did videos on all the advantages of investing in Dubai. These activities kept me focused on my goal: to enlighten the world about the benefits of Dubai's liberal taxation laws.

I started receiving tons of DMs complimenting me about my videos, telling me that my social media account kept them motivated or inspired them to join the real estate industry. This kind of feedback was great. It gave me the energy to continue in this way and to share more information.

Facing your fears is part of the journey to becoming a better version of yourself. Entrepreneurs must constantly reinvent themselves. Only when you challenge yourself can you know your potential. So go ahead and test your limits. Take Action!

STEP OUT OF YOUR COMFORT ZONE

To be very honest, when I started doing social media videos— whether it was a property video, a walkthrough, or educational videos—I never thought that it would be so successful or make this much impact. As a matter of fact, I always felt very shy talking in front of a camera. I was always so worried about how it would look and what people would say about it. The fact is that people will always talk about you no matter what you do, but this should not stop you from taking charge, going all in, and taking action.

It is really funny how these social media videos all started. Let me take you back to pre-COVID days in September 2019. I had traveled to London. While I was checking into a hotel, I was genuinely surprised by the low quality and standards of the hotel. Even though it was a huge brand name in a prime location, charging GBP220 per night, it was terrible. The hotel was nothing like what was advertised in the pictures, and the quality was the worst. It was such a shame for the brand.

The lobby smelled of fried fish, and the rooms were so tiny I could barely fit my bag. The hotel was dilapidated. It was disappointing to see the condition of the room. There were cracks in the thin walls between my, and the neighbor's rooms. I could hear him sing all night, and it wasn't a pleasant voice. The next morning, I went downstairs to complain to the staff.

I approached the receptionist, told her about my experience and disappointment, and explained that this was unacceptable. I even asked her if she could smell that awful fish odor in the lobby, and she told me, "You get used to it in a while!" She didn't even try to apologize or call a manager. All she said was that this was the hotel, and she couldn't do anything about it.

In other words, she was saying, "It is what it is. If you don't like it, leave!"

After living for so many years in Dubai, I got used to the impeccable service and luxurious conditions of this city. Never in my life did I expect that I would face that kind of despicable service and quality in London, especially after hearing so much about how fancy and posh the city was.

After I complained to the receptionist, I was furious, and that triggered me to pick up my phone and start recording a video. I shared my awful experience in that five-star hotel.

I wanted to highlight that people should appreciate what they are getting in Dubai, which is amazing and way more affordable than London. I even mentioned the service quality, the receptionist, and how unprofessional and rude she was. I detailed what Dubai has to offer in comparison in terms of customer service and an outstanding experience. I compared the two and posted that video without thinking of anyone's opinion because I was so pissed. I was letting off steam.

What happened next was a real shocker. I received nonstop DMs, likes, and comments, all agreeing with what I said. Many had faced similar experiences, and they even mentioned that Dubai was extremely underrated and had all the best luxury and service. I won't lie to you. It felt good to share, and that video was a great icebreaker with lots of people we followed but had never communicated with before. They were commenting on my videos.

BE PASSIONATE TO SHARE THE FACTS

Whether you know me or this is the first time you have heard about me, there is something I am very well known for, and that is my passion and obsession with real estate. I developed a very healthy habit of looking for properties no matter where I am on the planet.

To be the best or on top, you have to stay on top by getting as knowledgeable as possible and following every opportunity in the world.

That was the first thing I wanted to do in London on the second day of property hunting. I had gone to many different real estate shops and started getting information from them.

All that I can tell you is that I was extremely shocked by the sizes and the prices. They were more expensive than villas and mansions in Dubai. Few properties were freehold, most of what I saw was leasehold, and the stamp duty and property taxes were ridiculous.

So I started thinking that in Dubai, it is mostly freehold. You own your own parking space, which is not the case in London. You also have a gym and a pool in each building, with unlimited access, and you can bring whoever you want. The price of a five hundred square-foot one-bedroom in London can get you a four-bedroom villa in a golf course community in Dubai. In Dubai, you don't have to pay any registration because it is borne by the developer. Plus, developers in Dubai are offering that you pay forty percent over two years post the handover after moving in without requiring you to pay any interest on your money in a place where you don't pay any tax on your returns or capital gain. Dubai is one of the safest cities in the world, and you are still not happy about that?

I was, like, "What the hell is wrong with these prospects we are getting in Dubai? I think we are spoiling them as agents and entertaining their bullshit." That's exactly what I said in the video, and I posted it.

The fact is that Dubai sells itself. It doesn't need me. I just wanted to tell the world why to choose Dubai. That's when I came up with six bullet points. I shall share those in the next chapter.

Five minutes after I posted about my experience in London, my phone went nuts. People started resharing my videos, and I started getting DMs and comments. Some told me that I had no right to compare London with Dubai, and some told me that what I was saying made a lot of sense. Some agreed, and some disagreed, but the video created something for sure. It made a lot of noise, and that's the point of any video.

This time when I posted, it was not to let off steam—it was to share the value of investing in Dubai instead of London. It felt different. It felt like I was starting a debate. I was getting supporters, and I was getting haters.

Once that happens in your life, no matter what you are doing, know that you are doing it right. Do not fear haters. There will be people who will not like you, but that is their problem. You do what you feel is right.

While I was experiencing this in London pre-COVID, I waited for a couple of hours, and I made a third video. I clearly said that I wasn't comparing the two cities and that I was in London because I was hosting a property show in Mayfair for two days on the weekend from morning to evening. I mentioned the location and added that everyone was welcome to come over and have a look at the properties and learn more about the real estate market in Dubai. I said we were giving away lots of exclusive offers on the spot. I posted it and went out with the team for a nice dinner. I knew that, for the next thirty days, we were going to be hammering the phone and scheduling meetings.

It is important to understand how I work to create a buzz. Passion is the key element. There is no time for anything else when I plan a road show. Let's jump into the wild ride!

CHAPTER 3
PLANNING A PROPERTY ROADSHOW

"In any project, you give 110 percent with honesty."

– Anthony Joseph

L et me explain to you how this London roadshow event worked. We always scheduled the event on Saturday and Sunday from 10 am to 10 pm in a hotel venue or a boutique. The Dubai developers provide us with the area models, along with screen displays that rotate and show videos of the communities of Dubai.

To share how we organize the event, let's say the event is scheduled for the thirtieth and thirty-first. Before we travel, we start by contacting marketing companies on the fourteenth and then start generating leads. We then fly to London on the twenty-fifth. It is a seven-hour flight, so on the first day, we rest and settle, then we spend the twenty-seventh, twenty-eighth, and twenty-ninth calling those leads and leads from our own data, inviting them to the event and confirming the attendance and the numbers. This is the hardest part because, each day, we make between 150 and 200 reachable calls. We need at least ten to fifteen percent of those calls to become confirmed meetings to increase the chances of closing the deals.

As a team, we sit next to each other and start calling to get through these marathon calls. This creates such a vibe of energy in the room that it becomes exciting music to our ears. Even if someone gets tired, they won't stop because the vibe in the room keeps the energy levels high, which motivates them to keep calling as if their life depended on it.

When we finish on the third day, we compliment ourselves on the amazing job done and wish each other good luck. That day, we take it easy and have an early night. We need to be well-rested and build as much energy as possible for the next forty-eight hours.

I was very anxious and excited about my first event in a new place with new people, a new mentality, and a new approach. Everything was so new. It felt like a challenge, and that's what fires me up. I am always proving that I can take on a challenge any time, any day, and make the most of it.

The key is to imagine all the possibilities and be prepared for any situation.

I was extremely prepared. I had my iPad, which contained all the Google Drive brochures and videos available from Google Earth. I returned to check the videos I made to show the investment comparison between the two cities. I planned to meet and greet, have a quick chat, and sell the city straight away. The property comes last.

My goal was to first excite the client about the city.

Why Dubai? What makes it so unique? Why should they invest there?

I created six bullet points to talk about and then went for the kill.

I also invited investors to the roadshows. Trust me, when I used to tell them there was no tax, everyone was like, "It is too good to be true. There must be a scam!"

I would respond with, "These are the laws. I am not scamming you. There is zero tax, and purchasing property is simple. Even after selling, there will be zero tax on capital gains."

So that's how I was able to sell.

Here are my six bullet points of why Dubai is on the map of the world's best places to invest:

1. **Freehold.**

   Most of the properties in Dubai are freehold, and the buyer can be a single buyer or a joint buyer with their partner. Each unit comes with allocated parking that they can rent or sell. This property can be registered for inheritance in the Dubai International Finance Centre courts (following British courts). The landlord, his family and his visitors have unlimited access to the gym and swimming pool, free of charge.

2. **Tax haven.**

   Whatever property is purchased from me, I ensure that the developer bears this on their behalf, and I also offer property management services. This means we will be renting these properties, and they have to pay us nothing. All the rental income from the property is net to their pocket because Dubai, unlike the UK, has no tax on the returns. The investor can easily make six to seven percent net to their pocket on a yearly basis. Whenever they wish to sell the property, they don't need to pay tax on the capital gains, which makes investors happy as this is what discourages them and puts them off investing.

3. **The square footage price.**

   It's no secret that Dubai is extremely underrated compared to the major cities in the world, but compared to London, it's beyond explanation. I mentioned earlier the price of a one-bedroom apartment is equivalent to a four-bedroom villa in a golf course community. The price of a studio in London is equivalent to any three-bedroom apartment in Dubai.

4. Finance.

We have multiple methods of payment to accommodate any client and facilitate the purchase, such as the following payment structures: twenty-five percent during construction, seventy-five percent on handover, and twenty-five percent paid in twenty-four months; twenty-five percent during construction, twenty-five percent on handover, and fifty percent paid over two years without any interest, making it extremely easy to leverage the money; and twenty percent each year over five years, sixty percent until completion, and forty percent two years post-handover. We also offer the option of a bank mortgage of fifty percent. Even though this client has never been to Dubai, by paying fifty percent, the bank is willing to pay the remaining fifty percent for a maximum of twenty-five years.

5. Security.

The crime rate is generally very high in Europe, especially in the UK, but that's not the case in Dubai. It is one of the safest cities in the world. People leave their doors open and their cars unlocked, and women walk alone in the middle of the night, knowing they are safe.

6. **Weather.**

   Undoubtedly Dubai has the best weather in the world. From October to May, it's perfect, and everyone loves to spend time in Dubai. It's sunny all year long, which is the total opposite of the UK, where it is always raining and gray. So people can spend six to eight months in Dubai, and when it gets really hot in the summer, they can fly back to the UK to enjoy the summer.

After talking about these points about why Dubai was the best place to park their money or even live, I couldn't describe the look on the potential investors' faces. Many were shocked, and some were in denial. Some said it was too good to be true, that it was nuts, which always made me burst out laughing. I would say, "Who can blame you after everything they are doing to you here? I would have thought the same."

Right at that moment was the perfect time for Google Earth. I would show them the community, the buildings, the apartment, the playground, the mall, etc., and then we would jump to the floor plan to see the layout and choose the view, whether it was the Water Canal, Burj Khalifa, the school, greenery, or another direction.

By this stage, the client was usually seventy-five percent convinced and happy with everything they saw and heard, but of course, they still had doubts. These doubts arose because they didn't live in the city and feared, "What if something went wrong? Maybe it's a new scam. What if I am the new victim?"

In Dubai, we don't face these kinds of issues for various reasons, such as we are one of the leading companies in the city and are very well known for our credibility. Most importantly, it is normal for us in Dubai to have just one meeting and close the deal. However, overseas, we are new people in town, and the mentality is different.

I wasn't worried about that. I knew it would be a challenge. I would not only succeed, but I would also destroy all doubts in style.

I have a habit of using humor in my presentations to make the prospects laugh. This helps them to relax and feel comfortable. I always talk to them as if they are friends I have known for a long time. I say, "Hey, is this information overload? Let's chill for a minute. You are sweating. Let me order you a fresh juice." The juice takes five minutes to come, but for them, it is a breather, and it will be a good five minutes to make jokes, chill, and relax.

I reassure them, "Now you must be thinking: what will happen if I purchase a property and they never build it? Or what if it got delayed? What if it is smaller than expected? And what should I do? Whether you are having those doubts or not, I am going to answer all of those questions so you can have clarity."

I want to make sure that they get all their answers. This is where transparency becomes relevant. I give them as many details as possible so that they understand the process.

I explain, "First of all, you need to know that every developer in Dubai must have an escrow account for each project they are building. Basically, they put twenty percent of the project value in it, and every purchaser pays directly to the escrow account, which is held by the Dubai Land Department (DLD). Now by law, this developer has the right to delay for one year. For example, if they said the delivery is in May 2022, they can delay it to May 2023. However, if they pass that period, they have to compensate you by waiving service charges or paying you interest on your money, and in some cases, they will give an equivalent of one year of rent."

I go into more detail with them by explaining, "The developer has to deliver what they have stated, and both parties sign on the sales purchase agreement. For example, if you bought a 1200 square-foot apartment and they deliver 1000 square feet, you can benefit with a major price discount on your unit, and you can even cancel it and get a full refund plus a penalty."

This point is important for the clients to understand that they will not get cheated.

I go on, "The Dubai Land Department is very strict on its rules, and they made them this way on purpose so they create trust with the buyers, giving them the opportunity to purchase properties remotely, nice and easy, without any headaches."

Of course, after stating all these points, I show the buyers all the articles and the proof. While browsing through pages, looking for the questions and answers section, I explain, "We promised earlier that there would be a gift on the day of the event. I was offering furniture gift vouchers valued at 10,000 AED, or 2400 USD."

That's the secret formula!

I have ticked every box, so it is time to take a copy of their passport, driving license, and physical address.

I announce, "Congratulations! You have just purchased a house in Dubai. An online link payment will come to your email. Pay the one thousand pounds to reserve the unit, and you can transfer the remaining later next week when you sign the reservation form."

This worked seventy-five percent of the time. The remaining twenty-five percent (where it didn't work) was not because there was something wrong or due to any misinformation, but because, no matter what you did, the investors would never buy a property without seeing it.

I was ready for that, so I would look them in the eye and say, "So, you are telling me that you loved everything, and you are convinced the only issue is that you want to see the property before buying it?" The potential client says, "Yes, that's correct!"

I reply, "Well, that won't happen on my watch. I won't leave you hanging like that, nor will I ever accept that you wanted a property, and I haven't done my absolute best to get it for you, so let me tell you what I will do. I will take from you 1200 pounds, and I will reserve two air tickets with two nights in Dubai so you can have a full tour of our community."

If they still look unconvinced, I continue, "Once you are there and close the deal, this token amount that you paid will be deducted from your installments, meaning the developer would have paid for your flights and hotel. If you wish not to proceed, your worst-case scenario is that you took your wife on vacation!"

I look at them, finish that offer with a big smile, and look at the wife to see her reaction. That's it! Deal done. There is no way that they won't accept it. This is a no-brainer. That's how we brought people to Dubai and closed deals.

This is the secret formula that everyone was trying to figure out. I was prepared with the knowledge and an honest approach. I never took no for an answer, but I listened to their doubts, and I took action when needed.

We became so good at sales that the developers were hiring us to do roadshows in London, and we ended up doing nine in the year until March 10, 2020. That was the last time. We returned to Dubai from London, and the lockdown happened.

CHAPTER 4
TAKE ACTION –
BE SHARP

"Information is free, but wisdom is priceless."

– Anthony Joseph

Selling is selling in any field. You just have to know the pulse of your customer. Their psychology and thinking patterns are important. Tips about these areas are shown in the upcoming chapters.

First, what is the psychology of an entrepreneur?

Entrepreneurs can be of two types. The first is the get-rich-quick type—the type who doesn't want to do the hard work. They want to trade stocks or crypto and become the next billionaire. These guys are quick to burn out. They are all about money, not relationships. The second category of entrepreneurs is those who have the drive and the hunger to create solutions, innovate, and build relationships. They have not figured out their direction yet, but they have the ambition and passion. These are the kind of entrepreneurs who will ultimately make it.

In my first book, Take Charge, I refer to the trinity of success. You have to feed your mind, body, and soul. Making sure your mind and body are sharp means keeping updated with the current global news.

If you follow my methodology, in forty days, you will see the results. After six months, you will be totally transformed.

So, no matter which field or industry you are working in or what product you are selling, when you take charge of yourself and your life, you will, in time, be able to take action in the right way.

The Power of Information

It is amazing how fast times have changed and how much information we can access. If you want to get ahead in life, practice developing an obsessive dedication to mastering knowledge. To be a great entrepreneur, you need intense hours of study and observation.

If real estate is my business, I must analyze all the market information and data. Data is currency.

I came up with this quote which I believe reminds us why it is vital to stay informed: "Data is as important as oxygen."

Follow it, do research, and be on top of your game to ensure the investors are making money.

Property Monitor is the place to learn. I shall share more about this resource in a later chapter.

Knowing your product is extremely important. At times, the client is at the crossroads of an investment. When you know your product, you can provide comparative data and offer a comparable market analysis. People want to see tangibles. They want to know what benefits they will get from their investments.

Imagine an investor comes to you, and you sell him a garbage bin for a million dollars, and the investor gets $100,000 or double-digit returns. He's going to buy it. The investor has no specific tastes. They generally don't care. All they care about is how much they put in and how much they get out.

PEOPLE RESPECT HONESTY AND KNOWLEDGEABILITY

It is important to understand first what drives your buyer. At times a couple will come to see a property, and I can tell right away that the wife is the one who can arm-twist her husband. She will be the one to convince him. I then speak to the wife and show her the kitchen, the barbeque space, and possible children's rooms. I then ask her what she looks for in a home. I care about their needs and want them to have a perfect home where they would enjoy their life.

Another key element is how you come across to the buyers. I am careful about how I dress and how I present myself. The impression you create can make a difference in developing trust in the buyer's mind. I am friendly and honest, and I like connecting with people from different parts of the world.

What else can I do to add value to the buyers?

Yes, business was great. I worked damned hard, and I closed deals. I had my trinity of success framework, which kept me sharp. All has been going well. It was fabulous. I continued with my social media posts to generate leads. However, that's not all. To keep up the momentum, I needed to have an advantage over others.

Let's face facts: Dubai is a small city, about nine thousand square kilometers in size, with a population of about four million. So imagine four or five thousand companies are doing exactly the same marketing by using Facebook and Instagram.

I knew this fact and had to focus on other ways to keep myself in action. I did things differently.

First, I didn't put all my eggs in one basket. I was very much invested in the financial world, in stocks, crypto, commodities, and others. However, I had a plan and a direction, and I lived by a disciplined routine.

My early mornings of exercise and then an hour of reading the news and articles from all over the world kept me knowledgeable and creative.

What is the point of reading all that unrelated stuff?

Well, the secret about being a broker, or even an entrepreneur, is that you have to keep your eyes and ears open. You have to be alert for opportunities at all times.

For example, there was an economic situation in Italy, and people were tripping on their money. I targeted Italy. First of all, there was a surge of people moving their money, and from what I knew about Italy, they had a fifty to sixty percent tax range. I explained to them, "Buddy, there's zero tax here in Dubai." If the Italian investor was unsure and couldn't trust me over the phone, I knew at least fifty Italians who had been investing with me since 2016, and they knew me well.

I asked one of them to speak with the guy. Later, the new investor called me back. He said, "Here, take my money!"

At the end of the day, you need credibility. Anyone could see that my social media had over two thousand posts and five hundred videos. There were pictures of me sitting with the royal family, doing testimonials about me. People knew that I was legitimate in Dubai. However, the guy from Italy had never heard of me nor communicated face to face. Naturally, there would be doubts.

Therefore, in my books, relationships and credibility are super important in building clientele.

Every day we read about the tension in Russia and Ukraine. When the news of the tension started, my marketing campaign was only focused on these two countries. And guess what? Russians and Ukrainians were the best investors in Dubai in the fourth quarter of 2022. While the iron is hot, one must strike.

Trends changed fast, and soon enough, the Russians sent in their boys. I could not compete with them. The point is, look for opportunities. I was the first to see the investment potential.

Learn to see different opportunities through different perspectives. Instead of setting your eyes on a single location, look for trends and make connections on how you can bring a solution to someone's problem.

Another experience of seeing opportunities happened when I read the news about a woman in France who was wearing a hijab, and she was treated with discrimination. There were negative reactions and lots of criticism about the culture of the hijab. The news about this was spreading. And guess what? I did my marketing and sold to French Algerians, French Tunisians, and French Moroccans. These Muslims were under pressure in France. For them, the safest place was Dubai.

When I look back at pre-COVID times, there were many opportunities to grab.

With the kind of marketing I was doing and the freedom to travel, I had done many different roadshows, scheduling forty meetings in two days.

Whether the people bought a property or not, they became extremely interested in the information I was sharing with them.

I had an answer to every question that they had. I even had the answers to every question they didn't have, and I was asking and giving them the answers.

After the events, I would be exhausted but extremely happy, not only with the amazing results we all achieved but also with the reactions I received from every meeting.

It was invigorating. We would go out and celebrate all night. The next day we would be ready to return to Dubai, our favorite city, not only because it was home but because we had great pride in talking about it.

I still remember that day. I could not stop reminiscing and saying to myself that if I had this kind of crazy impact on forty meetings by just presenting facts and knowledge, what would I do if I shared this knowledge that I obtained over the years on social media?

And that was the trigger to take action.

Who cares about what people think? They will hate regardless. I knew I had the courage to do what they couldn't. What did I have to lose? Well, nothing. However, I had a lot to gain.

That's how I want you to think. You are the only one responsible for your life, your future, and the quality of life that you will live.

If you put in all the hard and smart work, you will become your own luck, you will control your destiny, and most importantly, you will become and make everyone around you super proud. That feeling is priceless. So, roll up your sleeves, be brave, and TAKE ACTION!

CHAPTER 5
STEP UP – GET SMART

Some people tell me, "I'm sorry, I cannot do a video in front of the camera. I'm super shy."

I tell them, "You're a dinosaur. It's time to put your money where your mouth is and adapt. Do what you need to do to run a business!"

I offered a solution to help them get over their shyness. Something I followed was called self-assessment. I made it a habit to do it regularly.

Instead of journaling, I picked up the phone and video recorded how my day went. Had I given my all today? Maybe I hadn't given it my all, but whatever I hadn't done that day, I would do the following day. Just one minute of that. This was between me and myself. No one would see or hear it.

On the second day, when I did the video, I said, "Yesterday, I promised that I was going to do better today." I continued for the third day and kept going. You can do this, too.

Make a promise to yourself.

The most beautiful part of this self-assessment that ninety-nine percent of the people don't get is that, after a month of doing this, they become super comfortable being in front of the camera. Without them realizing it, they overcome their shyness and start doing the videos.

This is how to work the conscious and the unconscious together.

Get started with a simple message about what you want people to know about you and your product!

You've got to understand how to target your market so that you're looking for opportunities and connections, not just using a scattergun approach. That's the same as everyone else.

"Data is the new currency. The more you know, the more opportunities show up to make money." – Anthony Joseph

The most used social networking applications are Facebook, Instagram, LinkedIn, YouTube, and Snapchat. Except for Snapchat, I was using most of them. I know you might think that I missed TikTok. However, in 2019, TikTok wasn't as big or as well known as it was in 2022.

So before I started recording, I went to YouTube and searched for Dubai property investments. This led me to teaser videos from developers. There were a few videos on how to invest in Dubai, but nothing that I found eye-catching or informative enough to generate interest. That's when I knew exactly what I should work on. I focused on property walkthroughs and educational videos.

Amazingly, I found what was missing in the market. Then, I needed to think of the content and find a videographer that would take care of the shooting and editing. When it came to the content, I didn't really complicate it. I knew I couldn't read from a teleprompter because I would stumble, so I decided to keep it real and freestyle. If I was doing a property walkthrough, I would just talk about what I saw. If I did an educational video, I would explain slowly and easily so that anyone watching that video would get the message clearly.

My strongest audience was on Instagram. I had around fifteen thousand followers, but most of these were either friends enjoying the travel/lifestyle pictures I posted or simply people from Dubai. At the end of the day, I always posted something about this city. I am undoubtedly Dubai's biggest fan.

Most people ask me, "Tony, what's your secret?"

I always reply, "It's no secret. You do it all, and by doing it all, it will pay off."

For example, for the email marketing campaigns, I sent out ten thousand emails. Out of that, I received fifty inquiries, and I closed five. I made this my business model in a month. Then I did the same for Facebook and Instagram and received another five leads. I followed through with other methods too, which averaged twenty sales a month. These leads didn't always follow up on a sale. Some months, people were traveling, and no one looked at their emails in the summer. You had to mix it all together.

This method was better than cold calling or cold texting.

LOOK FOR GAPS

When I moved to Dubai in 2014 and started my real estate training, we had to register with the Real Estate Regulatory Agency (ReRa). The Dubai Land Department was where we studied all the laws, regulations, and practices in the Dubai real estate market. It was the most informative course anyone could take. After going through it, I found that it was beautifully created to secure investors and tenants in such a way that it allowed people to park their money without having anything to worry about. Unfortunately, no one knew anything about it.

Tada! That was my Aha moment! I could make endless content about this gap in information.

When addressing an audience, the best thing you could do was to come up as the specialist, and they would definitely engage with you even if they were not a live audience. In order for that to happen, you need to understand human behavior and the human mind.

Before going into the psychology of a buyer, let us first understand what were the requirements to qualify as a broker. Then we should go into the workflow and responsibilities.

A broker is a licensed person who acts between parties such as owners, buyers, sellers, and even tenants. The broker could represent both parties, but the important fact had to be that the broker was super transparent with both parties about every other real estate transaction.

A broker must be a specialist or expert in his area and field. This means it is a high priority to provide correct information, not just estimations or projections. Luckily, concrete data from the Dubai Land Department is accessible to everyone.

When a broker does not have an accurate answer to a question, the broker has to be honest and tell the client,

"I am not sure. Let me find out," rather than just giving an answer which might affect the decision of the buyer and lead to another issue that could backfire in the near future.

I still remember the day I joined the ReRa course in 2014. It was like yesterday. I was filled with a sense of excitement, and I was hungry for knowledge. I was glued to the screen for those three days. The fact that I was taking this course and examination was a turning point in my life. It was the moment I had been waiting for.

Let me share a bit more of the context behind this excitement.

There was a point in my life when I was so broke and so poor that I had two options: commit suicide or do what I'm doing. Seriously, I had reached a dark space in my mind where I was doubting my presence. I was thinking to myself, why am I even alive? What's the purpose of my life? I was that disappointed with myself. I felt like, if a car had hit me, there was no emergency contact person. I would disappear from the face of the earth.

I was also super tough on myself. When I used to walk for long distances, I would get so exhausted I couldn't feel my knees. I would say to myself, "You deserve it, you piece of shit. You have been spending your money all your life. This is your punishment." So I was super harsh on myself.

That was my rock bottom. It was the worst place to be.

Frankly, you do need to hit rock bottom to rise from the ashes. There was no way that someone with any sort of comfort in life would be able to do something with that kind of grit. To get to that level of action, you must hit the floor and realize that "where I am today is my fault and responsibility."

People tended to blame the world, their country, or even their parents. They would blame everyone except themselves.

So focus on your life and purpose. Then fire up, take charge of your life, and then take action.

How can you change your life? Take a pen and paper and start putting a plan together. Then practice it over and over again. You will fail multiple times, but the only way is to keep going, and eventually, you will find the perfect formula.

So, for me, the perfect action was getting my broker's license. It meant a lot to me.

We received full training about Dubai's laws, rules, and regulations. It was overwhelming but very exciting at the same time, and I was ready to do my exam and get my broker's certificate and license.

It wasn't as easy as it is today. For someone to get the license, a person needed to be registered under a company first and then attend four days of training with the Dubai Land Department, which was then followed by an exam that an individual must take between seven to fourteen days of completing the course. The exam comprised fifty questions, and two points were given for each right answer. There were two different passing grades. The owner or the sponsor mentioned on the trade license needed a grade of only sixty percent to pass, while all other individual brokers needed a grade of eighty-six percent to pass. Any examinee who failed was given one free exam within ten working days.

Failing the second exam led the examinee to two scenarios:

1. If the examinee achieved a grade of seventy percent and above on their second exam, then they needed to pay $900, attend the course again, and then they would receive the certificate upon finishing the course.
2. If the examinee received a grade lower than seventy percent, then they had to pay $900 to attend the course again, take the exam for the third time, and achieve a passing grade in order for them to get the certificate.

The results were received immediately after completing the exam. Upon passing successfully, the certificate was printed on the spot.

This license is renewed annually and must be applied for at least thirty days before expiry. The process is easy. The applicant must register for an exam, pass it, and renew their broker ID for another year.

In 2019, ReRa announced that agents that had already passed their examination in the past five years would not need to renew their ID cards. They would be renewed automatically with the company's trade license.

In 2021, ReRa decided to stop this mandatory learning. Now, all brokers need is to start working under a company to receive their license and Broker Registered Number (BRN) through the trainees system e-services (www.dubailand.gov.ae)

This card means a lot to me. I worked hard and struggled for many years to get that ReRa card. I take pride in my work and recognize the value of my brokerage license.

It has been an honor for me to be a broker in Dubai.

I didn't expect people to be as obsessed as I was, working sixteen, eighteen, or even twenty hours a day. It's not healthy. However, you do what you have to do to get what you want.

I did what I had to do to build my reputation.

As long as you separate yourself from the people who tell you that you cannot make it or who say that it was pure luck that you made it big, you will grow. Stay away from such people who put you down.

Focus on developing yourself. Read books and articles. If you cannot read, get audiobooks and learn from videos. Nowadays, there is so much information, and most of it is free.

When I started, there was nothing.

It's amazing how fast times have changed, and our access to information is at our fingertips. You can get so many nuggets of wisdom.

Practice and develop yourself, and become obsessive in mastering yourself.

There is no academic path that can teach you what I know today. I learned from the streets, as we say, from practicing and making mistakes, from paying the price of failing.

All these experiences are beautiful. They taught me many lessons.

I have a proven record of offering the perfect service with perfect transparency. My company, called Anthony Joseph Management Consultancy, manages over 450 properties in Dubai. We offer expert opinions on business tasks and projects, risk management expertise, business planning assistance, and real estate or Dubai-specific consultancy. More than half of the landlords live abroad. I created an online platform called the host log where they can monitor all their tenants, bookings, how much money they are generating, and other information.

My clients shared with me what they wanted to do with their returns. Some wanted me to send them their money, some wanted me to pay my service charges, and others said they wanted to reinvest in Dubai. Managing these properties and landlords is not an easy day-to-day job. I do my best to ensure that all my clients are satisfied.

We are ranked the third largest company. Two of my competitors are bigger. One has been around for eighteen years and the other for eleven. I've been here for three years. However, like I told my competitors on a live video, I'm destroying them!

I have recently started a real estate academy called Take Charge Academy. I offer live courses on a weekly basis. I have partnered with the best trainer in the city. He's mature and a fatherly figure. I am young. Together, we make a balanced team.

Besides the Academy, I have a consultancy for anything related to any service for anyone who wants to invest or settle in Dubai. We have the knowledge, experience, and ethics.

My journey as an entrepreneur has taken me through many stages. In each stage, I noticed the market gaps and built my company like an umbrella to offer all the needs under one roof.

The world has changed, and we need to change with it, including how we are viewed in the world.

In the next chapter, you will understand the value of social media in enhancing your reputation.

CHAPTER 6
SOCIAL PROOF

*"Nowadays, your social media ID
needs to be stronger than your CV."*

– Anthony Joseph

If anyone wanted to know anything immediately about you, what would they do?

They would Google you or go on social media sites. These sites have billions of users per day. Being visible made a huge difference for me. A business profile is necessary, and you need to update and share what you are doing. If you made a sale, post it.

If I made a sale, it would be beneficial in two ways. First, if an owner stumbled upon a post showing that I had sold exactly the same property they owned, he would text me to say, "Hey AJ, how much did you sell that property for?" After telling him, he would respond, "I have the same unit on a higher floor. Can you get me more? If you can get me more, you make the sale."

This mode of communication broke barriers. There was no need for small talk, and people liked to get to the point.

My social media appearance has become extremely important. I never knew who might be watching my videos. Any of the views could lead to an opportunity for me.

So celebrating sales, celebrating another happy investor, or celebrating any kind of win, were the kinds of social proof that grew around me. People could see that I was the kind of person who could get results, and people knew I could be trusted.

I am reminded of an incident. I recall a salesgirl who worked in a retail shop and had nothing to do with real estate. She had seen me and my videos. She was aware of what I did, so she texted, "Hi. I know some people that are coming to Dubai. They want to invest. I cannot think of a better person than you. Will you do it?"

I was like, "Yes, let's meet up with them." From there, the investors purchased a property worth fifteen million.

I gave the salesgirl a referral fee of $20,000. Her annual salary was $17,000, and she made more than that from just this one deal. She was so grateful that whenever she heard someone wanted to buy property, she would tell them, "I know the best guy who can help you."

You never know who is watching, so make sure you are visible on socials.

THE GOOD AND THE BAD EXIST IN THE SAME MARKETPLACE

One point that I have to mention is that there are people who would offer a helping hand, but eventually, they fade away after they take the investor's money.

Despite the DLD's regulations, many times, people who came to Dubai got cheated.

Therefore, other laws in Dubai were developed that protected the buyer—Trakheesi.

What is Trakheesi?

Simply, it is an Arabic Licensing system, like a center for whatever you need from which you can obtain a permit. These permits helped curb false and duplicate real estate investments in Dubai. Trakeesi is mainly used by real estate professionals.

Trakheesi is a web application for real estate officers managing real estate brokerage operations. It was created to streamline the real estate industry, offer a range of key services for real estate professionals in the Emirates, and offer smart real estate services for brokers and real estate companies. These services included licensing permits and e-cards.

The DLD aimed to streamline and regulate various transactions and procedures for real estate professionals.

Let's dive into the services that real estate professionals could utilize on Trakheesi.

Apply for Permits for Property Advertisements

It is mandatory to have a marketing permit to publish any property advertisements in Dubai, meaning a Trakheesi permit is required for a property listing to go live on real estate portals.

Trakheesi permits are necessary to advertise a property in the following media:

- newspaper advertisements
- real estate promotional stands
- printed advertisements
- advertisements by SMS
- promotional stands
- promotional campaigns
- launching real estate projects
- real estate seminar permits
- open days
- advertising boards

- classified advertisements
- electronic advertisements.

This permit helped curb false and duplicate real estate advertisements in Dubai and ensured that all advertised properties were sold or leased with the legal owner's permission.

There are six steps to generate a Trakheesi permit.

Step 1: One of the requirements to apply for a Trakheesi permit is an advertising format, which is easily done through the management systems of the portal. Create a new listing draft and the relevant information about the property, such as the title and description, and upload the photographs. The owner must provide a No Objection Certificate for the advertisement or a Form A from the DLD.

Step 2: Log in to your Trakheesi account. Real estate professionals usually have their accounts under the business owner (your Dubai broker account).

Step 3: Click on the Trakheesi in the first menu. It directs the user to the Trakheesi dashboard.

Step 4: There are four menus on the Trakheesi dashboard:

- License—View the (user's) real estate agencies' DLD License
- Permit—Apply for Trakheesi Permit
- Warning—View all warnings that have been issued
- Fines—View all fines issued to the real estate agency.

Click on "permit" to apply for your Trakheesi permit.

Step 5: The permit page features a table that details all the previously approved Trakheesi permits.

Click on "add property," which then opens a dialogue box displaying five types of properties:

- project
- land
- building
- villa
- unit.

Choose the correct type of property, and fill in all the necessary information. This required information includes the following:

- area
- building name
- unit number
- municipality number.

You could always refer to the property's title deed to find this information.

On typing in the building's name, a drop-down menu will appear that displays a list of properties with similar names. Choose your building and then click on "search".

A new section to fill in more information will open up. Fill in the necessary information, including the following:

- purpose—rent or sale
- price from the price to—the price range of the property
- project number (this is used exclusively when applying for a Trakheesi permit for projects)
- amenities (this is optional).

Once you have completed this process, click on the 'save' button at the bottom of the dialogue box.

Usually, the Trakheesi permit applications have an automatic approval option enabled, which means you can instantly see the property's name on top of the table on the permit page.

You can see the Trakheesi number under the "Permit #" column of the property you have added.

Step 6: Head over to the draft of your property listing, and add the Trakheesi number. Voila! That's how you get your listing permit, and you can advertise it using any medium you wish.

APPLY FOR A REAL ESTATE LICENSE

The real estate business in Dubai can only operate with valid licenses. So, whether you want to start a brokerage or set up a consultancy, you must procure the relevant license that permits you to operate legally. Trakheesi Dubai deals with the issuance and renewal of a variety of licenses for real estate companies to operate in Dubai. These include free zone, developer, and deed licenses.

The following entities in the real estate sector can obtain a license from the Trakheesi system in Dubai:

- mortgage consultancies
- mortgage brokers
- consultancies
- developers
- leasing and selling brokerages
- real estate services trustee
- exhibition organizers
- owner association management
- real estate management supervision
- valuation services
- property inspection
- leasing and management (self-owned)
- leasing and management (others)
- real estate representatives.

The Trakheesi online system is also integrated with Dubai's economic development for a seamless user experience. It automatically syncs the license data between the databases if there are any modifications in the licensing information.

How can you apply for a real estate license through Trakheesi Dubai?

Take a look below at the steps to apply for a license for real estate companies through the Trakheesi system:

- Visit the Dubai economic department or free zone authority and submit your request.
- Once you have received approval, visit the official Trakheesi websites.
- Choose the register option.
- Fill in the required information and upload the necessary documents.
- Print the approval form.
- Visit the deed or free zone authorities with the approval form and complete the rest of the procedure there.
- Log in to the Trakheesi website and update your trade license number.

The documents required and the fees payable depend on the type of license that the real estate company was applying for under "Activity rules". You can learn about the necessary documents, requirements, and applicable fees for different real estate activities on the official Trakheesi website.

Real estate brokers can also apply for the Trakheesi Broker Card through the system. Once the license is issued, brokers can conduct a variety of transactions online, reducing the need to visit the Dubai Land Department.

APPLY FOR A TRAKHEESI BROKER CARD

Brokers can also apply for e-cards through the Trakheesi Dubai system. Once applicants have logged in to their Trakheesi account, they can choose the relevant service and fill in the required information for the Trakheesi broker registration, including the following:

- personal photo
- valid passport copy or Emirates ID (must be under the same license)
- real estate practitioners course certificate
- good conduct certificate from the Dubai police addressed to the Dubai Land Department or ReRa

Once the payment is made, the permit will be issued within two working days.

I am a big fan of newspaper advertisements. They always bring me good leads that are converted into sales. When doing a newspaper advertisement, there are a few points that you need to remember:

- It is mandatory to use both English and Arabic languages.
- Off-plan properties must mention the name of the developer, the escrow's account number, the expected date for project completion, and the proposed service fee.
- The real estate brokers' and the brokerage's phone numbers must be mentioned in the advertisement.
- The real estate permit number must be mentioned in the advertisement.

View the Brokerage Office Ranking System

There is also a brokerage office ranking system that was introduced to HH Sheikh Maktoum bin Mohammed Bin Rashid Al Maktoum in Cityscape Global 2015. DLD announced it on the first day, as well as many services for the investor, such as the investment map, rental dispute center, and registration trustees.

DLD has requested all real estate brokers working in the Emirate offices to log in to the link in Trakheesi system offices (classification) to update the details in the system, specifically those related to the internal regulations of the office.

This step was taken to enhance the efficiencies of real estate service providers (brokers) in accordance with set policies for the real estate sector based on the strategic plan of ReRa by creating a ranking for brokerage offices that was applied in January 2016.

Four criteria were adopted for ranking brokerage offices: Gold, Bronze, Silver, and a general category.

RANKING CATEGORIES

GOLD CATEGORY
FROM 91% -100%

SILVER CATEGORY
FROM 81% 90%

GENERAL CATEGORY
FROM 0% 70%

BRONZE CATEGORY
FROM 71% -80%

Brokers are scored on five factors:

- experience
- number of transactions
- commitment to real estate regulations
- structure of the offices
- social works.

The score ranking will be weighted as follows:

- fifteen percent based on the experience of the firm and the brokers
- thirty percent based on the size of the transactions carried out
- forty percent based on their adherence to DLD regulations
- ten percent based on the structure of their organization
- five percent based on their community activity.

CRITERIA AND WEIGHT OF EACH ASPECT

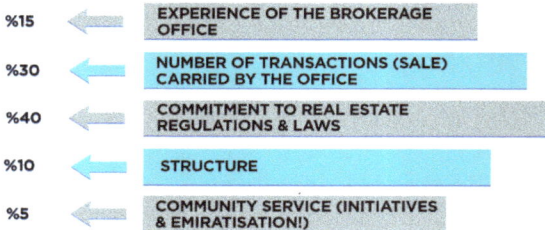

%15	←	**EXPERIENCE OF THE BROKERAGE OFFICE**
%30	←	**NUMBER OF TRANSACTIONS (SALE) CARRIED BY THE OFFICE**
%40	←	**COMMITMENT TO REAL ESTATE REGULATIONS & LAWS**
%10	←	**STRUCTURE**
%5	←	**COMMUNITY SERVICE (INITIATIVES & EMIRATISATION!)**

FIRST CRITERIA: THE EXPERIENCE OF THE BROKERAGE OFFICE (15%)

EXPLANATION	WEIGHT	YEARS	STANDARDS
THE POINTS ARE GIVEN FROM THE DATE OF OBTAINING THE LICENSE	1 POINT	1 - 5 YEARS	BROKERAGE OFFICE EXPERIENCE
	3 POINTS	5 - 9 YEARS	
	6 POINTS	10 YEARS	
THE POINTS ARE GIVEN ACCORDING TO THE AVERAGE YEARS OF EXPERIENCE OF WORKING BROKERS	1 POINT	1 - 5 YEARS	BROKERAGE OFFICE EXPERIENCE
	3 POINTS	5 - 9 YEARS	
	6 POINTS	10 YEARS	
	1 POINT	1 - 2	NUMBER OF BRANCHES
	3 POINT	3 - 4	
-	15	-	TOTAL

SECOND CRITERIA: NUMBER OF TRANSACTIONS (SALE) CARRIED BY THE OFFICE (30%)

THIS STANDARD IS BASED ON NUMBER AND VALUE OF SALE TRANSACTIONS CARTIED BY THE BROKERAGE OFFICE IN THE LD'S DATABASE AND ON MONTHRY BASIS

WELGHT	TOTAL NUMBER OF TRANSACTIONS
5%	+2
10%	+5
15%	+8
20%	+15

THE ABOVE SUB-CRITERIA REPRESENTS 20%

WELGHT	TOTAL NUMBER OF TRANSACTIONS
3%	2
5%	2 - 4
10%	4

THIRD CRITERIA: COMMITMENT TO REAL ESTATE REGULATIONS & LAWS (40%)

THIS CRITERIA IS CALCULATED BY THE NUMBER OF REGISTERED WARNING AND IRREGULARITIES COMMITTED BY THE BROKERAGE OFFICE

%15	WARNING
%15	O
%10	1-2
%O	+3

THE ABOVE SUB-CRITERIA REPRESENTS 15%

%25	IRREGULARITIES
%25	O
%10	1-2
%O	+3

FOURTH CRITERIA: STRUCTURE (10%)

THIS CRITERIA IS BASED ON FOUR SUB CATEGORIES

%	RESPONSIBILITY	EXPLANATION	SUB-CRITERIA	
%3	DARA AND STATISTICS SECTION	DOCUMENTATION OF SAFE RECONDS BY THE OFFICE	RECORD OF DEALS BY THE BROKER	1
%3	DUBAI REAL ESTATE INSTITUTE DIRECTOR	QUALITY SYSTEMS BY THE OFFICE (ISO)	QUALITY SYSTEMS	2
%2		-	DEDICATED WEBSITE FOR THE OFFICE	3
%2		-	MARKET CASE STUDY	4

NOTE: A SURVEY OF QUALITY SYSTEMS WILL BE SENT OUT TO BROKERS VIA EMAIL, ONCE WE RECELVE A RESPONSE WE WILL DECIDE THE GRADE

FIFTH CRITERIA: COMMUNITY SERVICE (5%)

WE PROPOSE TO MEASURE THE RANKING ACCORDING TO TWO SUB-CRITERIA

%	RESPONSIBILITY	EXPLANATION	SUB-CRITERIA	
%5	DARA AND STATISTICS SECTION	NUMBER OF EMIRATI NATIONALS WORKING IN THE OFFICE	EMIRATISATION	1
%5			INITIATIVES	2

"After studying all applicable standards, it will be issued a certificate of office by rating categories on the website, and gives the Office Card by four categories, gold star, or a silver star, or bronze or General Certificate star, and give a discount on course fees by 10% and 5% and 3%, respectively, while the ceremony is held to honor the winner of the gold category offices."[2]

Brokerages have categories, but brokers also check the following list:

- Blue Card—issued by brokerage companies licensed by DLD; allows brokers to transact in the Dubai free zone and sell for developers, but not timeshare properties.
- Green Card—issued by developers; brokers can only sell developers' projects.
- Red Card—only timeshare properties.
- Yellow Card—issued by brokerage companies licensed by a Free Zone authority and allows brokers only to transact in that free zone.

---

2   https://dubailand.gov.ae/en/news-media/dubai-land-department-showcase-the-brokerage-offices-ranking-system/#/

- Navy Card—issued for National Brokers.
- Gray Card—issued for registration Trustee.

HONESTY IS NOT ALWAYS THE BEST POLICY

The number one issue that people struggled with when they were looking to transfer to Dubai was, quite simply, honesty. When an investor moved to any country and planned to live there, lots of people offered help. "Yes! I will do this and that for you," they would say. They promised the moon until the investor made that payment, then blocked them and stopped answering their calls.

That was what I faced back in the day. Whenever I wanted to use a company's service, I found their service was terrible. I started looking for other companies, and they were even worse. So I said to myself, "You know what, Anthony? Instead of saying, 'these companies are bad,' why don't you create good companies?"

CHAPTER 7
ETHICAL ATTITUDE

So that's what I do—I help people set up in Dubai. My company is called 811 because we are the last step before 911.

We help with company formation, chief financial officer services (for those in charge of ensuring financial discipline, compliance, and internal control of the business), value-added tax registration and services, and other tax filing requirements. We even have a service to do a background check on any project or company.

For example, John came to me from New Zealand. He was looking to set up a second branch of his business. I guided him through the process and ensured all the relevant regulations were followed, and he got the required licenses. It was a smooth transition for him. Soon, John became one of my top investors. He made a lot of property investments. He enjoyed tax-free returns and was soon moving his assets to Dubai. He introduced me to people in his circle, and I made a lot of sales from his referrals.

Another time, I was selling a one-bedroom apartment. I would make from it $30,000. A client, an investor, came to me and wanted a higher return. Yes, I could tell him if this was a good investment option. Then he might say he would be interested in a villa. If I sold him the villa, I could make $150,000. However, I knew that, as an investor, he would not make money on a villa. He would enjoy living in it, no doubt. However, because I knew his requirement was an investment, I would tell him that it was better to buy five one-bedroom units. The villa was not worth the investment. I could have easily sold him the villa, but I don't work like that. The investor had specific needs, and I listened to them. Based on that, he followed my advice. He could tell that it was not about the money.

There was no law stopping me from taking advantage of the investor, but these were the principles I followed.

My principle for doing business is simple, and I repeat it again: treat your clients like you treat your parents.

Maintaining this track record has earned me a reputation as someone that people can trust. As a result, I am doing a mega volume of sales.

"Life's a marathon, not a sprint."

– Phillip C. McGraw

Before going into fundamentals and techniques, there is something extremely vital that I want to address. I want you to really understand it, and implement it, not only in real estate but in your life as well.

The fact is that ninety-five percent of my clientele are my friends.

I am not an annoying salesman. I am a friend with whom you can go property shopping. The way I work is simple: If I wouldn't buy the property myself, I wouldn't sell it to you.

With that logic, yes, I lost money, but I never lost my reputation. I don't consider it a loss because strengthening my reputation is much more valuable.

THERE ARE STAGES IN ENTREPRENEURSHIP

When you first start out, you are chasing the sale. For example, when I was broke as hell, I was still new to the business. I didn't know the correct way to start selling a property. I tried to learn, but no one really gave me the right guidance. I just followed what the others were doing. I had no prospects and was trying my best to get clients.

One day, I got a call from an Italian lady. She wanted to see a unit. I showed her the apartment and was polite and friendly with her. I was not focused on just getting a sale. I was sharing some light-hearted conversation.

I am a chatty guy. It's just the way I am. The lady was okay with my jokes, and soon she said her husband was on the way to view the unit. As we waited, I continued to be chatty and lighten the mood. The husband finally came, and I was equally friendly with him.

The manager of the building was watching me from a distance. He was giving me angry looks. He gestured to me. I went to him, and he whispered angrily to be careful how I speak with clients. I asked him what his problem was, and the manager said not to be so informal with the couple. He Googled the Italian and told me that the guy was, like, a billionaire.

I had $5 in my pocket! I had nothing to lose by being casual and nice. I wasn't in awe of the guy. To me, he was like any other potential buyer. At that moment, I didn't care what happened. Things couldn't get any worse. I was just going to be myself—friendly and honest. I was in the shittiest time of my life, but I still had the courage to face another day. I wasn't about to put up a false front.

Guess what? My friendly behavior and transparent approach won the deal! That was my first rental.

That's how I made it in the real estate world—with an honest, transparent approach toward the buyers.

Being yourself in how you talk and treat people and being genuine in understanding their needs was what made the difference.

The fact is that when times are tough, never give up. Know that you are being shaped the way you are meant to be, and embrace it. There is only one way, and that's up.

Every sale is an emotional roller coaster. You have to hit your buyer in his mind and heart. Speak to the person and the family so you can connect with respect, and they can picture their children and their lifestyle needs. Create a feel-good atmosphere with the client.

Before we get into the details of psychology, let me share with you the foundation of a real estate broker.

It is important to be clear about who you are and your principles.

In the next chapter, you will learn that unethical business practices are commonplace. I will share some typical ways that people get conned.

A daily reminder: Treat your clients like you would treat your parents.

I hold myself to a higher standard than I hold anyone else. It is important to deal with clients with honesty and transparency and by owning up where others would probably blame-shift or cover up their mistake.

The point is that I became the best and most honest at what I do. Anyone who is in the business would know it well.

For an entrepreneur to understand it, let me explain what I am—a broker who does a service between two parties. The simple way to look at it is that entrepreneurs notice the problems in life and provide solutions for them.

Trust is a key element because, from there, reputation is built. If the pillars of trust and honesty don't exist, reputation can easily be killed.

CODE OF ETHICS

First, let's understand what is a code of ethics and code of conduct and how to implement them in the real estate industry.

Codes of ethics and professional conduct outline the ethical principles that govern decisions and behavior at a company or organization. They give a general outline of how employees should behave and specific guidance for handling issues like safety and conflict of interest.

A code of ethics is broad, giving employees or members a general idea of the types of behavior and decisions that are acceptable and encouraged at a business or organization.

In most cases, businesses combine both documents into one, as there are significant overlaps between them. It is rare to find businesses that have two separate policies. While they are technically different documents, employees would have less difficulty recalling important points around conduct and ethics if they had a single document to refer to.

How does the code of ethics work in real estate?

At the end of the day, a code of ethics means being a good human being. That's it. It's not complicated.

That is the mission statement of the consultancy I have created so that new investors can get the correct guidance on the laws and regulations of the city.

The number one thing that people need to be aware of is who is legitimate and who's taking them for a ride. The key is to do your research and have someone trustworthy that you can ask. Find someone with a proven track record.

CHAPTER 8
LEAD GENERATION

"Your whole presence on the internet is lead generation."

– Anthony Joseph

The biggest misconception in our industry is that it is very hard to generate leads, and you have to indulge in marketing to do so.

Wrong!

It is not hard at all to generate leads. You just have to learn how to do it and whom to target.

Before the pandemic, after watching my regular online videos, many people came to the roadshow out of curiosity, and many left as owners of a property in Dubai. It was a great way to attract potential buyers.

When I returned home to Dubai, my wife complimented me on the videos I had made. She said I looked very natural on camera and should do them more often.

I was touched by her compliment. I replied, "Thank you, sweetheart, for all of your support. That's what I have been thinking about all day, how to make more content."

Before COVID-19, the cost per lead was about $40. During the COVID-19 pandemic, it went down to $7. It was crazy. It was an open market for us brokers, and we did crazy sales. All the companies went all in, like animals. We rated fifteen times higher than the regular days because no one was marketing. It was an open market for us.

All that I needed to do was get the right product, market it in the right way, and close deals.

Lead Generation – the Next Generation of Marketing

I want to share with you an example of the power of social media.

A quote by Beyoncé applies to my experience: "If everything was perfect, you would never learn, and you would never grow."

This is exactly how I lead my life. We learn, then learn more, and grow.

Beyoncé indirectly helped get me clients.

How?

This was what happened. I saw an Instagram post on someone's page. It was about the opening of the Atlantis, a world-class resort, where Beyoncé had sung for forty-five minutes and made $25 million. There were many comments and opinions about the event. Some were good, some were bad, but that didn't matter to me. What mattered was that Dubai was mentioned.

I added a comment: "For anyone who wishes to have a residence in the same building where Beyoncé performed, let me know."

That was one sentence. I got five inquiries. I made one sale.

While everyone was talking about Beyoncé, with some saying she was underpaid or overpaid, I couldn't care less. I watched the news to see the opportunity, not the gossip.

Focus on the stuff that matters, then take action!

> *"Small minds discuss people, average minds discuss events, and bright minds discuss ideas."*
>
> – First Lady Eleanor Roosevelt

This was my start in my social media life, and that's how I knew how important it was to target specific areas. Many people make the mistake of hitting too wide and targeting people who are not even interested in investing.

For example, if you are sitting at home, and I came to you with a product that you didn't even know or want, you would look at me as an annoying salesperson. With lead generation, there was a need, and we filled that need by providing solutions.

In all the noise of the internet, there will be duplicates. You cannot be unique. However, what you share could turn out to be educational. The information that you share can benefit someone.

Think about it this way: we are all consultants and experts in our field, and we are just giving away information to one person. However, what if you can give that information to five thousand people, and what if ten thousand people watched it, and so on? It is that simple. You would never know who might reach out to you.

Let's start discovering the many methods and how to use marketing and make it work for you.

EMAIL BLAST

This was my most successful method. My conversion ratio was really high. I can safely say that it was and continues to be between fifteen and twenty percent. Many servers provide email blast services. My favorite is Mad Mimi. I like it because it is user-friendly, and it is easy to customize the email format and graphics.

First of all, when uploading the email lists, make sure the list is clean (i.e., each email is correct and there are no typos). It is very critical that your bounce rate is very low.

Second, you can name the email sender whatever you wish. For example, if you are emailing for product X, you can name yourself X so that the receiver would immediately click without thinking that it was coming directly from the developer and not from a brokerage or individual broker.

Third, the title has to be very eye-catching. It is the most important factor that attracts people to click and open the email. It is what we refer to as clickbait.

Fourth, share limited information. The less you share, the better because you want them to get curious, so they will reach out for more information.

Keep it simple, with an eye-catching title image, limited info, and a WhatsApp button to direct them to your number.

Use an email tracker that will tell you exactly when the email was opened and how many times the recipient looked at it.

There are five scenarios that might happen when the recipient receives your email:

1. They will call you.
2. They will WhatsApp you.
3. They will reply to your email.
4. They will ignore your email.
5. They will block you.

In the first three scenarios, the prospects are interested in getting more information. This means they have an appetite, regardless of whether this specific product is suitable. This is a perfect way to qualify and put them in a specific category to help you close the deal.

Although not impossible, it is rare that a prospect will buy the same product you send them.

The email list to which you send your information might contain a first-time buyer, an end-user looking for his forever home, an experienced investor, someone with multiple units but who is out of cash, or many other interested people. Your qualifications and skills lead to a sale, which is what we call conversion or a converted lead.

The common mistake that could happen is overdoing email blasts or thinking that sharing more data will lead to more responses. This is not necessarily so. The best way is to treat your list like a baby. First, send an email to two thousand people at a maximum, and after a few days, to five thousand people, and keep it this way to maintain your connection. Overdoing it will lead to your account, and sometimes your IP address, being blocked.

SMS Blast

For this service, you can send as much as you want on the server, but keep in mind that people often abuse this mode of marketing. People barely look at SMS these days unless it is something really important or interesting.

So how can you maximize the use of SMS marketing?

Create a landing page where it mentions your services and what you do. It can include relevant information about a specific product or specific service. It can also have a nice video in it.

When you blast this SMS, you should make sure that they need to open the link, so you should put a triggering sentence, such as "Attention Community X Owners," and below it is the link. When they receive the SMS, there is no way that they will not open it. It is not in their hands. It is their curiosity. When the SMS redirects them to your landing page, they will go through it and simply click on the WhatsApp button, which will redirect them to you, and the rest is on you to qualify and close them.

GMAIL EMAIL ADVERTS

This is the simplest way to advertise. The recipient receives an email in the social category that says Ad on it, and when the individual clicks on it, they will open an image. Next to it, there would be some minimal information about the property.

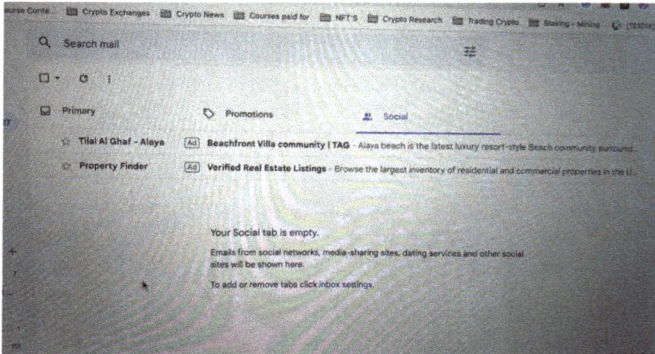

After clicking, you see some detail about the property and a link to visit the site to learn more.

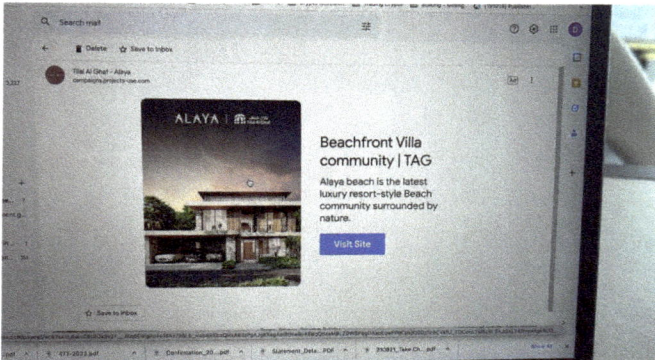

Facebook and Instagram Lead Generation

This is the most used form of marketing, and most companies do the same, expecting results without realizing that no one is really benefiting from this mode except Mark Zuckerberg. It is a very strong tool if you know how to use it correctly. For example, everyone does the same in Dubai by preparing the advertisement and targeting Dubai, the same location used by all. This makes the lead cost fly high without getting any quality leads.

YouTube and TikTok

These are similar concepts to Facebook and Instagram, but they are limited to videos only.

Most questions asked are about the best landing page builder, the best call to action button, or whether the press or check fund is best.

What matters more than anything else is having a great sales pitch that gets the attention of potential leads.

We have all heard the saying, "Seeing is believing." That's why I urge you to make the sixty- to ninety-second video. Be prompt, and make sure to perfect your pitch so you give this viewer no other opportunity but to click and inquire.

It is all a numbers game. If your video is viewed by 100,000 people, this means 100,000 chances of a stranger becoming a prospect. If it is interesting enough, they will share it with their circle of friends.

You might be asking yourself, "Who is the target audience?"

The answer is simple—"Anyone that's got money!"

The main mistake that agencies make is targeting people who have previously shown interest in real estate.

What I do differently is target a different audience. First, I choose both males and females. When it comes to age, the best range is between twenty-five and fifty years old. You can use any location that you wish. I target countries of wealth, such as Monaco and Switzerland, and countries with high tax rates, such as Italy, UK, Germany, and similar. I keep the cost per lead very cheap, and the chances of another agent competing on the same lead become very low.

This is the most cash-efficient way that works for me. Most importantly, this has the highest conversion rate without having to worry about an agent sacrificing his commission to steal the deal. Again, this will not work if you don't have the perfect sales pitch. So make sure to get the video done and go ahead and blast it.

WEBSITE

Get a killer website and a monthly Search Engine Optimization service where it will be ranked high, and make sure these are updated on a weekly basis. It is very easy to drive traffic on a beautiful website that looks legit and has eye catchy content, such as nice listings and videos.

PRO MAGAZINE

This method works under the condition of using a Class A magazine. This gives good leads and credibility, which separates you from the rest of the competition.

THE NURTURING

Nothing is stronger than the power of knowledge. You should give free knowledge to attract people. Always go live on Instagram, LinkedIn, YouTube, and so on. Explain to people the key benefits of investing in Dubai. Trust me. It works like magic. Once people understand why it is very beneficial to do so, they will start coming to you and referring you to their circle of friends, and that's what it is all about—being different, being knowledgeable, and being an ambassador to the industry and to Dubai specifically.

CHAPTER 9

KNOW YOUR PRODUCT

We can all agree that the world revolves around data, and data is the new currency. It doesn't matter if you are working in primary, secondary, or even commercial real estate. What matters is knowing the history of the area and the price movement in sales and leases because this exact data is the reason why people would or would not buy in that area.

There are lots of applications that share these kinds of data. My favorite is Property Monitor. I have been using it for years, and it has never failed to impress all the clients I have dealt with.

Before I start talking about its features, I want you to understand that I am not a shareholder in the company, nor do I know anyone working in it. I am not promoting it. It is just the most useful platform that helped me through the years, making crazy sales in Dubai.

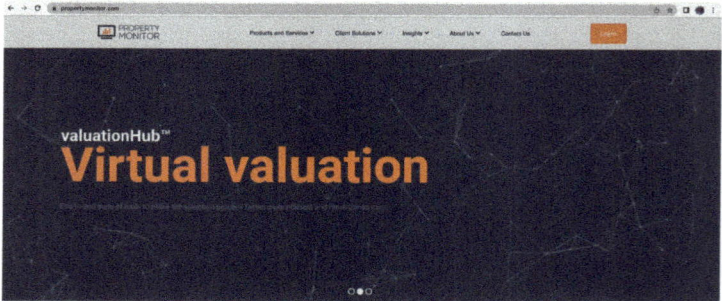

When logging on, the first thing you see is a moving banner that mentions all the areas. This includes showing the price movement as green or red with the percentage.

On the fixed banner, you have the first option, which is the heat map. It shows you the overall map of Dubai with seven color variations from the most popular to the least, including sales and rentals.

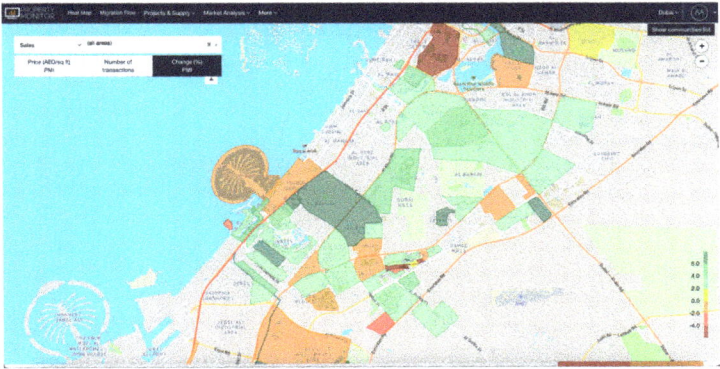

MIGRATION FLOW

This tool shows you the exact movement in and out, illustrated on the map with seven color variations. You can search by area and view if it is also listed. This tool is very useful and helpful for investors to guide them to understand where people are moving into so that they can invest in those areas and avoid the ones that people are moving out of.

PROJECTS AND SUPPLY

You get a fabulous overview of the Dubai map, the total number of projects, the number of projects in each community/city, the title type (such as freehold/ leasehold), the location, and the quality. It also lists the developer directory, where you can search any developer registered and see how many projects they have, their number of completed projects, and their phone number and email.

MARKET ANALYSIS

There are seven features in this category, which are concrete data that will get ninety percent of the sale done.

Market Statistics

Apartment

Select Bedroom

☰ Export

% Change

4.87 · 4.46 · 4.34 · 4.27 · 3.85 · 3.76 · 3.58 · 3.52 · 3.36 · 3.09 · 3.01 · 3 · 2.93 · 2.82 · 2.71 · 2.71 · 2.63 · 2.39 · 2.24 · 2.19 · 2.14 · 2.11 · 2.09 · 2.09 · 2.07 · 2.02 · 1.98 · 1.98 · 1.98 · 1.91 · 1.69 · 1.67 · 1.65 · 1.63 · 1.44 · 1.29 · 1.19 · 1.17 · 0.96 · 0.91 · 0.82 · 0.7 · 0.37 · -0.35

Al Kifaf Heights · Jumeirah Golf Estates · Al Sufouh · Al Hebiaa City · Al Barari · DAMAC Hills · Dubai Creek Harbour · Palm Jumeirah · Mohammed Bin Rashid City · Zabeel · Dubai Science Park Residence · Jumeirah Village Circle (Dubai South) · Business Bay · Al Furjan · DIFC · Dubai South · Jumeirah Lakes Towers · Dubai Sports City · The Hills · Emirates Living · Downtown Dubai · Meydan · Dubai Hills Estate · Dubai Marina · Dubai Studio City · Barsha Heights (Tecom) · Town Square · Motor City · Al Barsha · Arjan · Dubai Silicon Oasis · Liwan · Dubai Residence Complex · Jumeirah Village Triangle · Dubai Production City · Bluewaters Island · Living Legends · Remraam · City Walk · Dubai Festival City · International City · Dubai Investments Park · Culture Village Apartments · Discovery Gardens

Property Monitor.ae

Sr. #	Evidence Date	Development	Community	Sub Community	Beds	Property Type	Annualised Rental Price	Contract Rental Price	Built-up Area (sq ft)	Plot Size (sq ft)	Rent (AED/sq ft)	Unit No.	Rental History
1	30 Apr 2023 / 29 Apr 2024	Discovery Gardens	Mediterranean Cluster	Building 95	1	Apartment 5110001	42,900	42,900	958	-	45		Renewal
2	30 Apr 2023 / 29 Apr 2024	International City	Morocco Cluster	Block G	1	Apartment 6210001	31,000	31,000	716	-	43		Renewal
3	30 Apr 2023 / 29 Apr 2024	Deira	Al Muraqqabat			Apartment 1240675	32,890	32,890	344	-	95		Renewal
4	30 Apr 2023 / 29 Apr 2024	Bur Dubai	Al Souk Al Kabeer	Cyber House Building	3	Apartment 2450511	69,000	69,000	1,807	-	38		Renewal
5	30 Apr 2023 / 29 Apr 2024	Bur Dubai	Al Karama		2	Apartment 3180875	74,000	74,000	1,612	-	46	402A	Renewal
6	30 Apr 2023 / 29 Apr 2024	Jebel Ali	Jebel Ali 1		1	Apartment 5110001	42,900	42,900	990	-	43		Renewal
7	30 Apr 2023 / 29 Apr 2024	Muhaisnah	Muhaisnah 4	Al Wasl Building 502	Studio	Apartment 2450436	19,200	19,200	200	-	96	108	Renewal
8	30 Apr 2023 / 29 Apr 2024	Layan Community			3	Villa 6665385	133,345	133,345	3,947	3,947	34	C-31	Renewal
9	30 Apr 2023 / 19 Jan 2024	Emirates Living	The Views	The Fairways	2	Apartment 3881480	98,186	71,000	1,453	-	68		Renewal
10	30 Apr 2023 / 29 May 2024	Meydan	Manazel Meydan		2	Apartment 6180897	118,000	118,000	2,124	-	56	114	New
	30 Apr 2023					Apartment							

112

Apartment

Area	Type	Price					
Al Barari	Apartment	1,355				-1.51%	4.71%
Al Barsha	Apartment	966	0.82%		-5.01%	-5.71%	-3.83%
Al Furjan	Apartment	838	-0.95%	-1.04%	0.37%	1.04%	-0.30%
	Villa	941				-0.25%	
Al Habtoor City	Apartment	1,818	20.65%	34.55%	50.23%	24.00%	7.46%
Al Khail Heights	Apartment	593	4.56%	16.32%	2.96%	0.98%	0.20%
Al Sufouh	Apartment	1,000	2.77%	-3.58%	-2.18%	2.75%	-1.20%
Arabian Ranches	Villa	1,302	11.84%	9.04%	3.73%	6.43%	1.63%
Arabian Ranches 2	Villa	1,214	14.02%	13.22%	9.28%	4.46%	2.65%
Arjan	Apartment	862	5.75%	0.94%	-1.86%	0.64%	-1.13%
Baraha Heights (Tecom)	Apartment	846	0.00%	-18.26%	24.96%	10.36%	-6.17%
Bluewaters Island	Apartment	3,663	27.69%	19.19%	4.12%	2.77%	-2.94%
Business Bay	Apartment	1,487	0.52%	2.78%	4.78%	3.57%	1.27%
City Walk	Apartment	1,766	3.44%	1.54%	5.47%	1.52%	3.04%
Culture Village	Apartment	1,057	4.46%	12.89%	23.57%	2.57%	0.91%
DAMAC Hills	Apartment	1,028	8.01%	9.27%	0.00%	1.38%	0.46%
	Villa	1,169	10.49%	7.58%	3.98%	-0.10%	-0.89%
Discovery Gardens	Apartment	554	11.55%	9.91%	13.22%	7.96%	3.12%
Downtown Dubai	Apartment	1,879	15.21%	8.65%	6.70%	4.71%	2.94%
Dubai Creek Harbour	Apartment	1,740	-3.50%	-4.07%	-5.69%	-2.49%	

Dubai Land Department Residential Total Sales Volume / Total Sales Price - Transferred Sales (Title Deed) vs. Off-plan

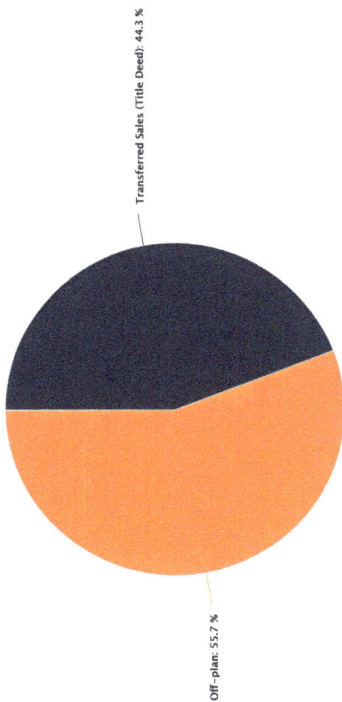

Transferred Sales (Title Deed): 44.3 %

Off-plan: 55.7 %

Residential Sales Volume - Transferred Sales (Title Deed) - Dubai Land Department in March 2023

Dubai Land Department Commercial Sales Volume - Transferred Sales (Title Deed) vs. Off-plan

01 Jan 2023 - 25 Apr 2023

* Click on the graph to drilldown

Transferred Sales (Title Deed): 78.6 %

Off-plan: 21.4 %

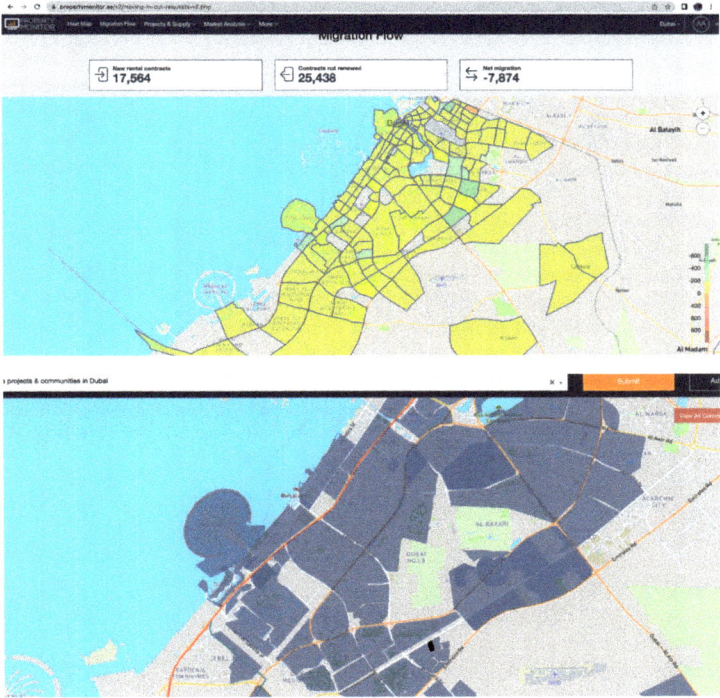

You can go back in time as needed and use this data to show your investors how much it has appreciated since the launch and how much room the area, project, or product still has to grow.

Sales Transaction Analysis

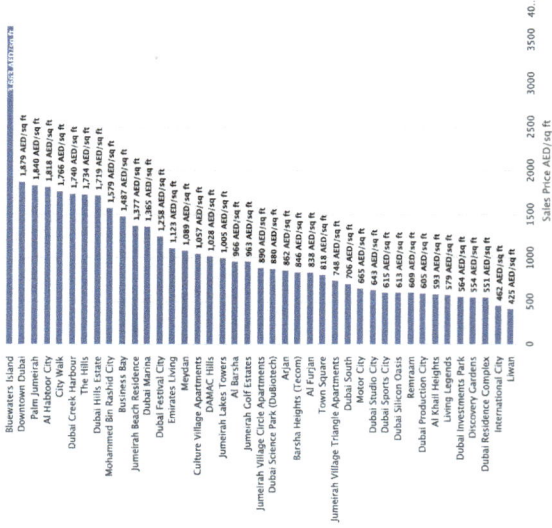

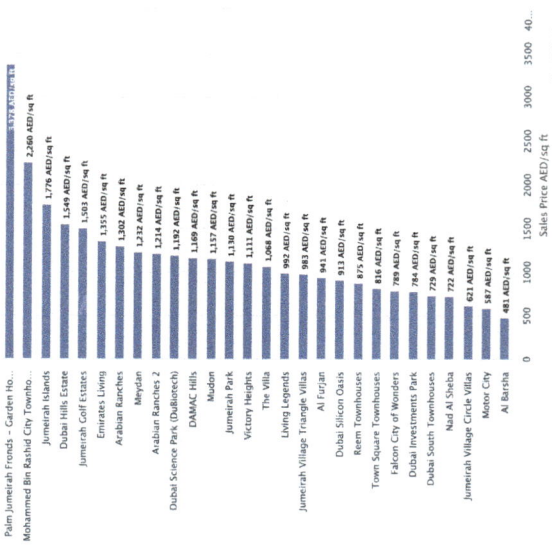

Villa/Townhouse

Select Bedroom ▶

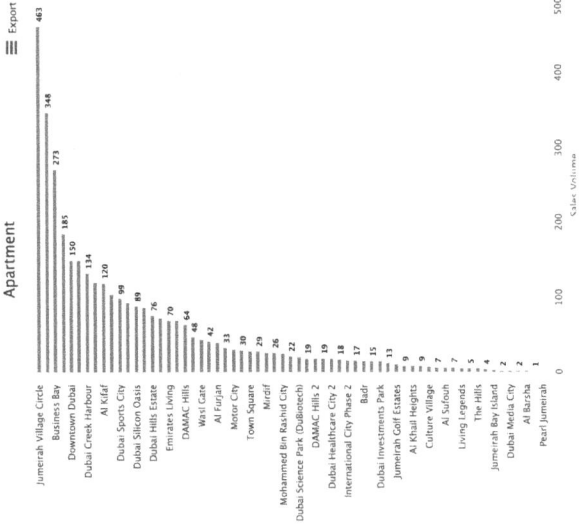

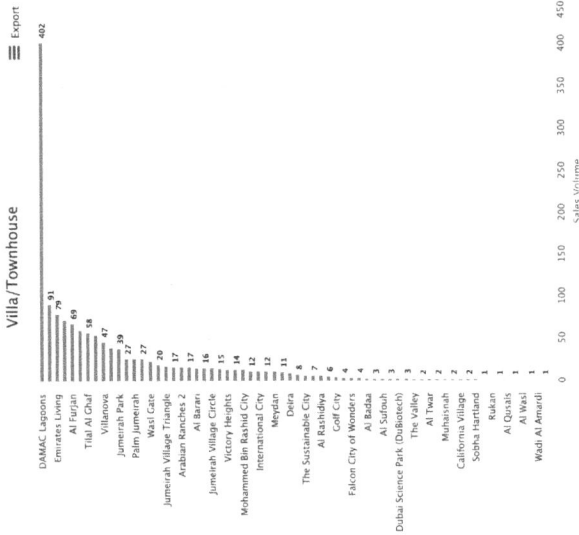

≡ Export

Location	Sales Volume
DAMAC Lagoons	91
Emirates Living	79
Al Furjan	69
Tilal Al Ghaf	58
Villanova	47
Jumeirah Park	39
Palm Jumeirah	27
Wasi Gate	27
Jumeirah Village Triangle	20
Arabian Ranches 2	17
Al Barari	17
Jumeirah Village Circle	16
Victory Heights	15
Mohammed Bin Rashid City	14
International City	12
Meydan	12
Deira	11
The Sustainable City	8
Al Rashidiya	7
Golf City	6
Falcon City of Wonders	4
Al Badaa	4
Al Sufouh	3
Dubai Science Park (DuBiotech)	3
The Valley	3
Al Twar	2
Muhaisnah	2
California Village	2
Sobha Hartland	1
Rukan	1
Al Qusais	1
Al Wasi	1
Wadi Al Amardi	1

Sales Volume (0, 50, 100, 150, 200, 250, 300, 350, 400, 450): 402

Apartment

Select Bedroom ▶

≡ Export

Location	Sales Volume
Jumeirah Village Circle	463
Business Bay	348
Downtown Dubai	273
Dubai Creek Harbour	185
Al Kifaf	150
Dubai Sports City	134
Dubai Silicon Oasis	120
Dubai Hills Estate	99
Emirates Living	89
DAMAC Hills	76
Wasi Gate	70
Al Furjan	64
Motor City	48
Town Square	42
Mirdif	33
Mohammed Bin Rashid City	30
Dubai Science Park (DuBiotech)	29
DAMAC Hills 2	26
Dubai Healthcare City 2	22
International City Phase 2	19
Badr	19
Dubai Investments Park	18
Jumeirah Golf Estates	17
Al Khail Heights	15
Culture Village	13
Al Sufouh	9
Living Legends	9
The Hills	7
Jumeirah Bay Island	5
Dubai Media City	4
Al Barsha	2
Pearl Jumeirah	2
	1

Sales Volume (0, 100, 200, 300, 400, 500)

119

Rental Analysis

Total Rent per Bedroom

01 Apr 2023 - 25 Apr 2023

Type	Total Rent (AED)	No. of Contracts	Average Rent (AED)	Average Rent (AED/sq ft)
Studio	97,470,805	2,854	34,152	88
1 Bed	3,628,258,692	6,795	533,960	651
2 Bed	430,960,109	6,597	67,360	64
3 Bed	213,924,978	1,820	117,541	62
4 Bed	82,426,015	438	188,187	88
5 Bed	30,998,413	111	279,265	47
6 Bed	4,675,833	14	333,988	31
7 Bed	2,220,000	3	740,000	41
8 Bed	1,440,000	2	720,000	34
9 Bed	150,000	1	150,000	120
10 Bed	4,760,000	2	2,380,000	63
13 Bed	25,000	1	25,000	47

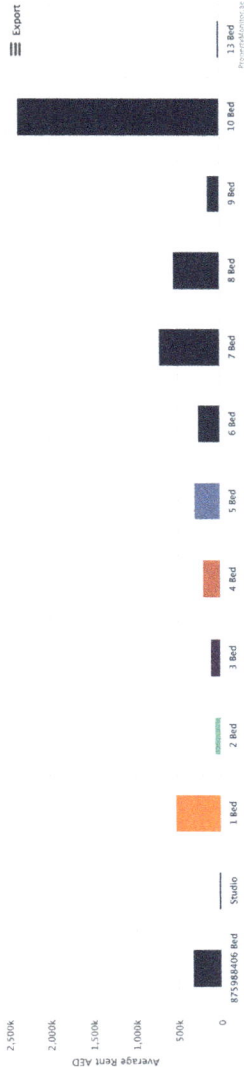

Average Rent per Bedroom

* Click on the graph to drilldown

≣ Export

Average Rent AED

2,500k
2,000k
1,500k
1,000k
500k
0

875 988 406 Bed · Studio · 1 Bed · 2 Bed · 3 Bed · 4 Bed · 5 Bed · 6 Bed · 7 Bed · 8 Bed · 9 Bed · 10 Bed · 13 Bed

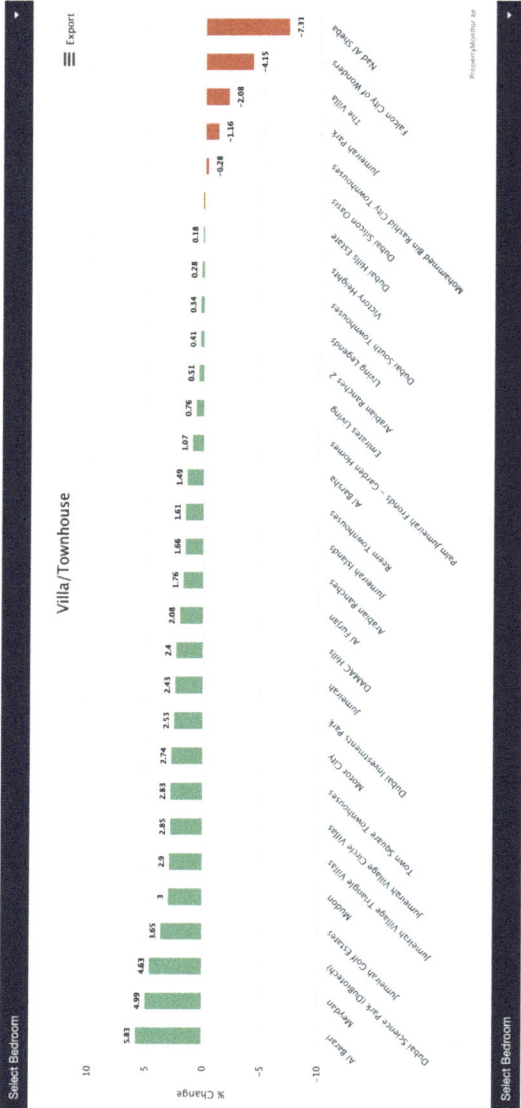

Change in Residential Rental Price from February 2023 to March 2023

Villa/Townhouse

Commercial Sales Analysis

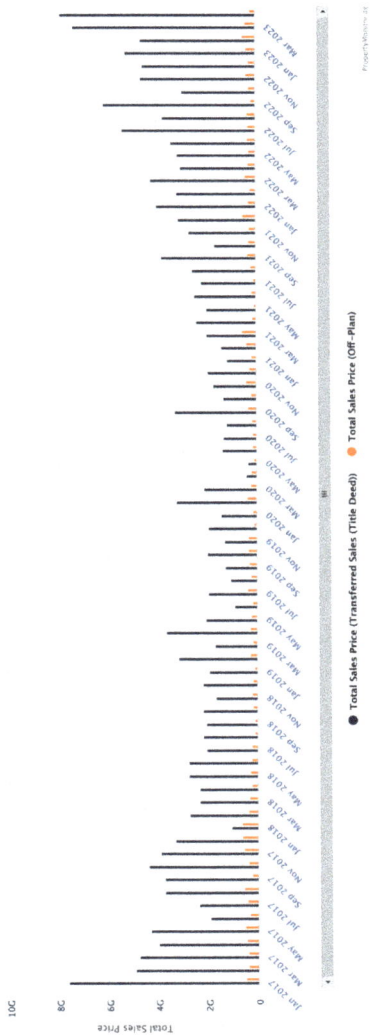

Dubai Land Department Commercial Total Sales Price - Transferred Sales (Title Deed) vs. Off-Plan

Commercial

* Click on the graph to drilldown

● Total Sales Price (Transferred Sales (Title Deed))   ● Total Sales Price (Off-Plan)

Developer Comparison

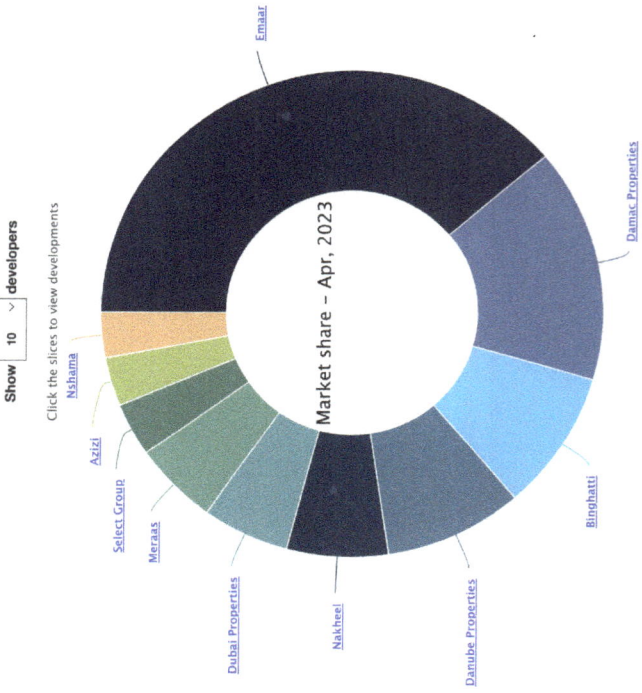

Developers Transferred sales (title deed)/Off-Plan sales volumes/values (DLD)

Show 10 ∨ developers

Click the slices to view developments

Market share – Apr, 2023

Emaar

Damac Properties

Binghatti

Danube Properties

Nakheel

Dubai Properties

Meraas

Select Group

Azizi

Nshama

Name	No. of transferred sales (title deed)/off-plan sales	Total volume rank	Total sales (AED)	Total sales rank	Total built-up area (sq ft)	Average sales (AED)	Average built-up area (sq ft)	Average sales (AED)/sq ft
Emaar	1,378	1	4.01B	1	1,767,933	2,906,909	1,389	2,060
Damac Properties	662	2	1.06B	3	736,863	1,621,371	1,644	1,209
Binghatti	326	3	246.92M	10	268,306	757,426	823	968
Deyaar Properties	316	4	272.13M	9	221,345	861,155	700	1,250
Nakheel	232	5	849.48M	4	365,890	3,661,582	1,929	1,513
Dubai Properties	198	6	452.03M	6	314,205	2,282,977	1,786	1,300
Meraas	195	7	1.21B	2	315,173	6,187,610	1,650	3,165
Select Group	124	8	302.89M	8	119,101	2,442,495	960	2,297
Azizi	114	9	89.63M	24	67,372	787,939	596	1,405
Mahaleia	109	10	114.06M	19	114,174	1,046,460	1,097	980
Sobha Group	80	11	154.62M	15	70,037	1,737,268	914	1,836
Majid Al Futtaim (MAF)	81	12	596.04M	5	95,596	7,235,080	3,063	1,194
Ellington Properties	81	12	161.69M	13	79,454	1,996,172	980	1,752
Seven Tides	99	14	103.23M	21	78,424	1,496,068	1,136	1,825
Deyaar	66	15	64.6M	25	58,218	978,788	682	1,123
Dar Al Arkan	59	16	62.86M	26	64,879	1,082,039	1,099	946
Samana Developers	58	17	51.38M	28	41,295	885,461	711	1,374
Wasl	50	18	107.42M	20	60,803	2,148,307	1,216	1,703
AG Properties	48	19	22.57M	49	26,465	470,261	551	861

Dubai House Price Timeline

Dubai House Price Timeline – Sales Price AED
January 2008 – March 2023

Indices and Trends

	Total Volume	Total Rent Price (yearly)	Total Built-up Area (sq ft)	Average Rent Price	Average Built-up Area (sq ft)	Average Plot Size (sq m)	Average Rent (AED/sq ft)
Overall	25,235	5,036,170,580	31,829,946	199,571	1,342	39,928	239
Apartment	23,092	4,657,539,022	26,433,160	201,695	1,172	-	248
Villa	1,766	328,225,296	4,481,465	185,858	5,630	48,521	122
Townhouse	377	50,406,282	915,321	133,704	2,494	3,860	52

Dubai City Index - Sales

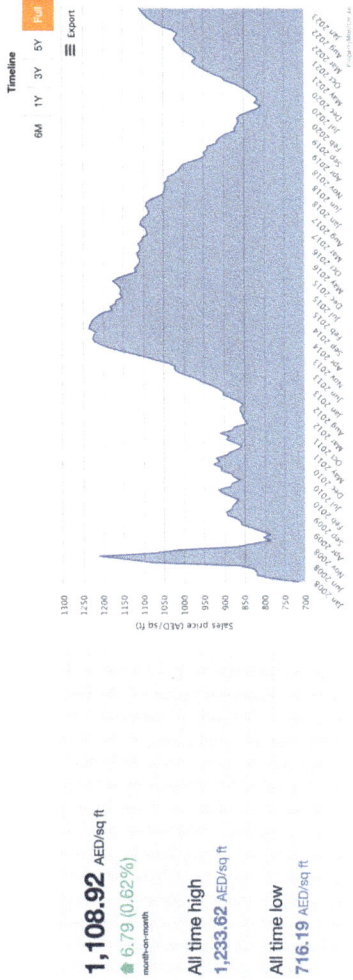

1,108.92 AED/sq ft
▲ 6.79 (0.62%)
month-on-month

All time high
1,233.62 AED/sq ft

All time low
716.19 AED/sq ft

Timeline
6M 1Y 3Y 5Y Full
≡ Export

Sales price (AED/sq ft)

Select month: March 2023

Reports
- Comparative Market Analysis
- Communities Price Trend Report
- Market Analysis Report

Data
- Building/units Data
- Population Distribution

Tools
- Service Charges
- Lease Date Calendar
- Lease Creator

CLOSING STATEMENTS

"Data is as important as oxygen."

– Anthony Joseph

"It's not a sprint; it is a marathon."

– Tony Robbins

CHAPTER 10
THE HUMAN MIND

"Hit your buyer in his mind and his heart."

– Anthony Joseph

Transferring excitement for your product from the salesperson's mind to the buyer's mind is the secret to a successful sale.

The sales process is an emotional experience. The buyer must see the value in his mind and feel the benefit.

The evaluative process used by the buyer is a logical one. This means the buyer is looking for facts, conducting research, comparing and evaluating various options, and then following through an elimination process before selecting the product.

The selection is based on comfort and attachment after the evaluation. This is the emotion that influences the ultimate decision.

Since thinking and feeling are mental processes, it is important to understand how the right and left brain work.

The brain is divided into two parts: right and left. The left brain is the logical, practical, and rational side, while the right brain is the emotions, feelings, and relationships side.

How can you identify a left-brain type of behavior?

The left brain dominates buyers' minds. They like to be in control. They are very specific in their statements. They are detailed and continue to look for value in terms of outcomes. They like organization, structure, effectiveness, and fact-based approaches.

The left brain is divided into two thinking profiles:

1. The Challenger—These prospects rely on the top left part of the brain to make decisions. They are aggressive and impatient, love to take control, look at the big picture, and focus on the end result. They like facts that are summarized and a selling approach that focuses on the benefits which are presented efficiently.

   Challengers are high risk takers. They evaluate quickly and make immediate decisions based on key facts. They like tangible results and prefer working with salespeople who demonstrate confidence and competence and are results-oriented.

   When communicating, they tend to tell rather than ask. They speak loud, fast, and interrupt to get quickly to the desired information.

   Challengers' conversations will demonstrate short statements to the point, with minimum focus on detail.

2. The Organizer—These prospects operate from the bottom left part of the brain. They are sequential and

structured and tend to initiate the approach. They need a high level of information and demonstrate good attention to detail. Organizers prefer a planned, logical approach that does not miss steps but addresses all the information in detail.

Organizers make their decisions after careful research. They check the validity of information and proof of all information presented.

Organizers tend to ask many questions about the details and only make decisions after checking all possible alternatives, and they prefer tried and proven progress. They are soft-spoken, patient, highly attentive, and think carefully before speaking or responding.

The right brain is divided into two thinking profiles:

1. The Responder—This refers to the right, bottom-brain thinking approach that makes them focus on how they are feeling during the process. Responders are friendly, warm, cooperative, potential, and loyal. They value

the relationship and professional interest shown by the salesperson. Responders dislike pressure selling tactics and prefer third-party references and testimonials when deciding to buy. When you are presenting to responders, use their names. They often use words like we and our rather than I and you. After presenting opportunities, it is important to give Responders time to express their feelings. They feel threatened by strong, aggressive selling approaches. Responders are uncomfortable with a logical and fact-driven approach. Responders prefer community, lifestyles, who's buying, and family-based approaches, and they like sellers being warm and who come across as being friendly. They don't like being rushed and don't like conflict. Therefore, they would not voice concerns, meaning that they are unlikely not likely to open up and ask questions. The sellers must engage with Responders by asking good open questions to understand how they are feeling.

Once they have purchased a property, Responders are very loyal clients who will be able to refer other clients of a similar nature to the salesperson.

2. The Engager—Engager prospects prefer a thinking approach that uses the top right side of the brain. They are vibrant, energetic, real, and excitable. They gesture a lot and are facially very expressive. There is no focus or attention to detail. Their sentences are long and expressive. They are extremely influential, motivational, and impatient when they speak, but there is no structure, organization, or planning in their approach.

Engagers quickly lose interest if the sales conversation becomes dry and boring and is filled with details, facts, numbers, and research.

Engagers like to be excited. When they make buying decisions, what matters to them is the product's look and feel, brand association, and status enhancement.

Engagers will make a buying decision based on usual representations. They are highly imaginative and can picture the community and how it will function in the future.

When selling to an Engager, excite them by involving them with personal stories. Let them speak about their achievements, and do not interrupt them while they are talking about what matters to them.

Engagers are principally self-centered. Therefore, they like their egos to be massaged, so do recognize their achievements and appreciate them. With a minimum focus on detail, Engagers are willing to close the deal with the salesperson. They like jokes, they like humor, they speak loudly, and they are fast, but they are long-winded, they interrupt, and they want to take control and shift the focus of the conversation to themselves.

When selling to people with these different personality types, it is important for the salesperson to be able to recognize the preferred thinking style and the behavior being demonstrated by the prospect. "People buy from people who are like themselves."

Let's recap.

People who are **left-brain** thinkers are practical, logical, factual, sequence structured, and organized, with an attention to detail, and they are very effective and efficient in their approach. They do not build relationships on friendliness and warmth. Instead, they build relationships, comfort levels, and trust based on effectiveness and efficiency.

Right-brain people are innovative, creative, influential, motivational, inspiring, friendly, cooperative, loyal, and trustworthy. They build relationships on interpersonal engagements and are motivated by details, structure, planning, and organization.

So, since people buy from people they like, and people prefer people like themselves, it becomes important for the salesperson to recognize the style of the buyer and change their approach to match the style of the buyer. In doing this, the buyer opens up faster, builds trust, and comfort easier, and it is a smoother process for the buyer to make a decision because he sees the salesperson as someone who is just like him or thinks like him, feels like him, and make decisions like him.

Front-brain buyers are loud and aggressive. They like to interrupt and take control with high energy, lots of movements, and gestures. If we see that type of behavior in a personality, the salesperson needs to mirror that. Become more confident and more assertive, use your hands and gestures, and have better eye contact because they like to work with those kinds of people.

Hindbrain buyers are softer and more patient. They speak slowly, they are calm, they do not interrupt, they listen very well, and they will tend not to ask questions.

For salespeople to engage with them, you need to slow down, be patient, and carefully think of the words you are saying. Do not match the hindbrain buyer. Instead, ask questions to encourage them to get into the conversation. Since they are patient, they do not interrupt. They don't work to take control of the interaction. They tend to work more from the inside, so we need to draw them out by asking good open-ended questions.

My note to any salesperson is to identify these combinations of the front, back, left, and right brain, then adopt the selling approach to match. In many cases, when the connection doesn't happen, it has nothing to do with the product or the opportunity. It simply has to do with the fact that two people are using different sides of their brains when trying to communicate with each other. Therefore, the whole-brain thinking approach recognizes the personality and simplifies the need and the budget they want to buy. It also identifies how they like to think and feel when making decisions.

Once you are able to identify this, it becomes easier to present the product and build trust. This then minimizes the objections because you are presenting in a way the investor is comfortable with, and this helps them make the decisions quicker.

Any salesperson who is looking to become a master of his profession must look to understand the left, right, front, and back brain and master identifying the four styles: the Challengers, the Organizers, the Responders, and the Engagers.

CALL TO ACTION

Life has changed multiple times. Generations evolve, and children follow their parent's way of thinking. They follow a conditioned lifestyle. The system that built mental slavery is broken.

Look at the world now. Eight billion plus people are connected through the internet. We have more access to data, and life has changed drastically. If you don't want to be part of the old system of thinking, then change. Opportunities exist everywhere.

If you want to live life on your own terms, then my advice to you is this:

- Learn constantly.
- Don't let divorced people give you relationship advice.
- It doesn't matter if your family says something that you don't like. You are not a tree. Go somewhere else.
- Adapt. Things are different now. Learn and grow from that knowledge.
- Trolling Instagram or other social media sites is good if you use the information to develop your skills.
- Change what you are consuming.
- Don't say life is tough.

- Life gives opportunity to everyone. What you consume is what makes or breaks you.

Go ahead Take Charge and TAKE ACTION!

Author Bio

Anthony Joseph is a self-made serial entrepreneur. He moved to Dubai in 2014 with only a few hundred dollars, but today he is one of the city's most successful and celebrated entrepreneurs and real estate agents. During his real estate career in Dubai, he has served many clients looking for short-term rentals, which served as inspiration for his company, Primestay. By recognizing the demand from the huge volume of tourists, investors, residents, and corporate clients seeking fully furnished accommodation, Anthony led Primestay to become recognized city-wide as the leading holiday home service provider. Along with their five-star quality service for both home and short-term leases, they offer housekeeping, laundry, and even VIP concierge services. If that wasn't enough, they've also added property management and interior design to their long list of expertise. In addition to his entrepreneurial successes, Anthony Joseph was named the best broker for 2018, 2019, 2020, and 2021 by major developers, such as Emaar, Dubai Holdings, Jumeirah Golf Estate, and many more. Anthony Joseph is the host of the podcast Dubai Stars. He is also an award-winning author of one of Amazon's best-selling books, "Take Charge".

Anthony holds a record sales volume of $1.3 billion in just four years. He is the co-founder and CEO of Primestay holiday homes and Prime Cleaning, the founder of Anthony Joseph consultancy and the Take Charge Real Estate Academy, the host of the Dubai Stars podcast, and an associate partner at Provident Real Estate.

SCAN HERE TO CONNECT WITH ANTHONY

NOTES